Money Management from Zero

A Clear and Practical Guide to Growing Your Wealth with Digital Tools and Small Initial Capital

ETHAN WEALTHMORE

Table of Contents

Chapter 1: Starting from Zero 4

Overcoming Money Myths and Building Financial Confidence 10

Chapter 2: Foundations of Financial Literacy 17

Essential Financial Concepts for Beginners 22

Chapter 3: Setting Realistic Financial Goals 29

Chapter 4: Tracking Your Money 32

Creating a Simple, Personalized Budget 35

Chapter 5: Digital Tools for Money Management 39

Choosing the Right Digital Financial Apps 41

Comparing Banking, Budgeting, and Investment Apps 43

Chapter 6: Saving Strategies for Small Budgets 48

Chapter 7: Building Wealth with Micro-Investing 51

Investing Scenarios with 10€, 100€, and 1000€ 55

Understanding Investment Risks and Rewards 57

Chapter 8: Avoiding Common Money Mistakes 59

Chapter 9: Building Credit and Trust with Banks 62

Building and Improving Your Credit Score 65

Chapter 10: Side Hustles and Digital Income Streams 71

Chapter 11: Protecting Your Money in the Digital Age 76

Protecting Yourself from Digital Scams and Fraud 79

Chapter 12: Emergency Funds and Future Planning 83

Setting Up Your First Emergency Fund 85

Chapter 13: Measuring Progress and Adjusting Plans 87

Chapter 14: Beginner Success Stories and Lessons 90

Chapter 15: Building a Confident Financial Future 92

Chapter 1: Starting from Zero

A young adult in their early 20s sits at a cluttered desk, the soft glow of a laptop screen illuminating their face, while empty coffee cups, crumpled receipts, and a bank statement showing a balance of $12.47 are scattered around. The atmosphere is tense, yet there's a flicker of hope in their eyes. This scene is familiar to many; countless individuals find themselves at a similar crossroads, pondering how to manage their finances effectively in a landscape that often feels overwhelming, especially when resources are tight.

One common misconception about money management is that it's only for the wealthy or those with formal finance training. This belief can be paralyzing, leading many to think that without a substantial income or a degree in finance, effective management is out of reach. However, this couldn't be further from the truth. **Money management** is a skill anyone can learn and master, regardless of their financial background or current situation.

Recognizing that money management is a skill is the first step in this journey. It's similar to learning to ride a bike or play a musical instrument; it requires consistent practice, patience, and a willingness to learn from mistakes. The key is to start with manageable tasks and gradually build your skills. For example, creating a basic budget using a free app like *Mint* or *YNAB* can be an effective starting point, helping you track expenses and analyze spending patterns, which is essential for making informed financial decisions.

A significant barrier to effective management is the mindset with which one approaches it. Many people operate from a scarcity mentality, focusing on financial limitations rather than available resources. This mindset can lead to fear-based decisions, such as hoarding cash or avoiding investment opportunities due to perceived risks. Shifting to an abundance mentality is crucial; it involves recognizing opportunities for financial growth and understanding that money is a tool that can be used to generate additional wealth, focusing on potential rather than constraints.

Technology plays a vital role in making financial knowledge and tools accessible to everyone. Today, numerous apps and online platforms help individuals manage their finances, invest, and understand complex concepts in a more digestible way. These tools are often free or low-cost, making them available to anyone with an internet connection. For instance, apps like *Mint* or *YNAB* offer user-friendly interfaces for budgeting and expense tracking, while platforms like *Coursera* or *Khan Academy* provide free courses on personal finance and investing.

To illustrate the impact of disciplined money management, consider the story of Chris Gardner, whose life was depicted in the film "The Pursuit of Happyness." Gardner started with nothing, facing homelessness and financial despair. Yet, through sheer determination and disciplined practices, he transformed his life by learning to budget meticulously, save consistently, and invest wisely, ultimately becoming a successful stockbroker and entrepreneur. His story shows that with the right mindset and tools, anyone can overcome financial adversity and achieve prosperity.

Exploring the potential of money management for everyone reveals that progress begins with a single action, such as:

- Establishing a basic budget
- Seeking out financial education resources
- Changing one's perspective on money

Each step contributes to building a solid foundation for financial growth. The path may present challenges, but with persistence and a strategic approach, financial confidence and growth are within reach.

The young adult, now more determined than ever, sits at their desk, exploring a financial education website filled with valuable information. They take notes diligently, eager to absorb the knowledge that will form the foundation of their financial management. As they scroll through the site, key terms that are essential to financial literacy catch their eye: **budgeting**, **saving**, **investing**, **credit**, and **debt**.

Budgeting is about creating a clear plan to allocate income effectively, ensuring there are enough funds for both essential expenses and discretionary spending. By meticulously tracking income and expenses, they can allocate resources strategically, preventing overspending and ensuring that financial obligations are met. A simple budget might categorize expenses into:

- Fixed needs, like rent and utilities
- Variable wants, such as dining out or entertainment subscriptions

The goal is to balance these categories to align with specific financial objectives.

Saving means setting aside a portion of income regularly for future needs, whether for an emergency fund, a major purchase, or retirement savings. Consistency and discipline are crucial for effective saving; even small, regular contributions can add up significantly over time, especially when taking advantage of compound interest. For instance, saving $50 each month at an annual interest rate of 5% can grow to over $3,000 in five years, highlighting the power of consistent saving habits.

Investing involves putting financial resources to work with the expectation of generating a return. Unlike saving, which usually carries lower risk, investing comes with a higher level of risk but also the potential for greater rewards. Common investment options include:

- Stocks
- Bonds
- Mutual funds

Understanding the risk-return tradeoff is key to making informed decisions that match one's risk tolerance and long-term financial goals.

Credit is the ability to borrow funds or access goods and services with the promise to repay later, playing a vital role in financial management by enabling significant purchases, such as cars or homes, that may be out of reach otherwise. However, managing credit responsibly is essential to avoid accumulating **debt**, which is the total amount owed to creditors. Effectively managing debt means making timely payments and understanding the terms of credit agreements to steer clear of high-interest charges and penalties.

Financial literacy is the cornerstone of effective money management, empowering individuals to make informed financial decisions that help them avoid common pitfalls and reach their goals. Setting financial goals is a crucial step in this journey, as they provide direction and motivation, shaping money management strategies. Whether it's saving for a vacation, paying off student loans, or building a retirement fund, having clear, measurable goals helps maintain focus and discipline.

Understanding one's financial situation is equally important, as it involves a detailed grasp of income, expenses, and financial obligations. A comprehensive view of financial health enables informed decisions regarding budgeting, saving, and investing. Digital tools can be incredibly helpful here; budgeting apps like *Mint* or *YNAB* allow for monitoring spending and setting financial targets, while online banking provides real-time access to accounts, making it easier to track financial activity and make necessary adjustments.

The young adult continues to explore the website, recognizing the importance of these concepts in building a solid financial foundation. With each note taken, they move closer to achieving financial confidence and growth. This journey is just beginning, and the next step is to investigate the strategies and tools that will help them reach their financial goals.

The young adult, now equipped with foundational knowledge, stands before a whiteboard, ready to outline a detailed personal financial plan. This visual representation serves as a structured guide, helping to navigate the complexities of financial management. The first step involves conducting a thorough assessment of their current financial status, which includes a careful evaluation of all income sources, such as:

- salaries
- freelance earnings
- passive income streams

Alongside a detailed inventory of fixed expenses like:

- rent or mortgage payments
- utilities
- insurance

As well as variable expenses such as:

- groceries
- entertainment

They must also account for outstanding debts, including:

- credit card balances
- student loans

And assess available assets, such as:

- savings accounts
- investments

Cataloging these elements provides a clear understanding of financial health, highlighting areas that need immediate attention and those that offer opportunities for improvement.

With a solid grasp of their situation, the next step is to set realistic and achievable financial goals that follow the **SMART** criteria: specific, measurable, attainable, relevant, and time-bound. Short-term goals might include saving $200 each month or eliminating a $1,000 credit card debt within six months, while long-term goals could involve accumulating $50,000 for a retirement fund or saving $20,000 for a home down payment within five years. Breaking these goals into smaller, actionable tasks helps maintain motivation and effectively track progress.

A key element of any financial plan is creating an **emergency fund**, which acts as a financial cushion against unexpected expenses such as medical emergencies, car repairs, or job loss. Ideally, it should cover three to six months' worth of essential living expenses, calculated based on the monthly budget. Building this fund requires discipline and consistency, often starting with small, regular contributions—like $50 per paycheck—that gradually add up over time. The peace of mind that comes with having an emergency fund is invaluable, as it allows individuals to handle financial setbacks without derailing their overall strategy.

Reducing expenses is another important aspect of financial planning, which involves a careful analysis of spending habits to identify areas where costs can be cut without significantly impacting quality of life. Practical strategies might include:

- cooking at home instead of dining out
- canceling unused subscriptions
- choosing generic brands over name brands

Implementing these changes frees up additional funds to direct toward savings or debt repayment.

Increasing income is equally vital for reaching financial goals, and exploring side hustles or freelance opportunities can provide a significant source of extra income. The digital landscape offers numerous options, ranging from:

- online tutoring
- graphic design
- selling handmade crafts
- offering consulting services

Leveraging existing skills or learning new ones enables diversification of income streams, enhancing financial stability and speeding up progress toward goals.

Ongoing education and adaptability are essential components of a successful financial plan. As circumstances change—whether due to fluctuations in income, shifts in expenses, or evolving personal priorities—the plan must be adjusted accordingly. Staying informed about financial trends, exploring innovative tools and strategies, and being open to revising goals and methods as needed are crucial. Adopting a flexible approach allows for navigating the ever-changing financial landscape with confidence, ensuring the plan remains relevant and effective.

The young adult, now equipped with a smartphone, opens an app designed to track expenses and set savings goals. This digital tool, with its user-friendly interface, transforms the often daunting task of financial management into a manageable daily routine. By entering each transaction, the app categorizes expenses and creates a clear visual representation of spending patterns. This immediate feedback helps users make real-time adjustments, keeping their financial goals within reach.

The digital landscape offers a variety of tools tailored to different aspects of money management. Budgeting applications like **Mint** and **YNAB** provide solid platforms for tracking income and expenses, while investment platforms such as **Robinhood** and **Acorns** allow users to start investing with as little as $5. Many of these platforms also include educational resources that guide beginners through essential investment concepts, covering a range of assets from *stocks* and *bonds* to *ETFs* and *mutual funds*. Financial planning software like **Quicken** or **Personal Capital** gives a comprehensive overview of an individual's financial health by integrating budgeting, investment tracking, and retirement planning into one easy-to-use interface.

Technology simplifies the process of managing finances by automating routine tasks, significantly reducing the chances of human error or forgetfulness. Automatic transfers to savings accounts ensure regular contributions, while automated bill payments help avoid late fees and support a healthy credit score. This hands-off approach saves time and reduces stress, allowing individuals to focus on long-term financial strategies instead of daily administrative tasks.

Digital investment platforms have changed the way people invest. With the introduction of fractional shares, even those with limited funds can invest in high-value stocks. This accessibility encourages **diversification**, a key principle in risk management. Spreading investments across various asset classes helps minimize potential losses and improve overall returns. Many platforms also offer **robo-advisors** that use algorithms to create and manage a diversified portfolio tailored to the user's risk tolerance and financial goals. This level of customization, once reserved for high-net-worth individuals, is now available to anyone with internet access.

The benefits of using digital tools go beyond convenience; they empower individuals to take control of their financial futures, fostering a sense of autonomy and confidence. By clarifying complex financial concepts and providing actionable insights, these tools enable users to make informed decisions that align with their personal values and goals. The young adult, now more confident in their financial management skills, begins to see the potential for growth and stability.

However, exploring the world of digital finance comes with new challenges. The convenience of technology carries inherent risks. Cybersecurity threats are significant, with hackers constantly looking for vulnerabilities in financial systems. The young adult, aware of these potential dangers, must navigate this digital landscape with caution. They start to question the security of their financial data, weighing whether the benefits of digital tools outweigh the associated risks.

While pondering this dilemma, a notification appears on their phone: an alert from their investment app indicating a sudden drop in the stock market. Anxiety sets in as they watch their portfolio's value decrease sharply. A critical decision looms: should they hold their position, trusting in their long-term strategy, or sell assets to minimize losses? The uncertainty is palpable, and the stakes have never been higher.

In this moment of tension, the young adult realizes that achieving financial independence involves navigating various challenges. The path ahead is uncertain, and the choices made now could have significant long-term effects. As they evaluate their options, a sense of urgency drives them to seek further knowledge and adapt to the ever-changing financial landscape. The next steps are crucial, promising new insights and strategies to effectively manage the complexities of money in the digital age.

Key Takeaway

Money management isn't just for the wealthy or finance experts—it's a practical skill anyone can learn, even with limited resources. By starting small, using digital tools, and focusing on building habits like budgeting, saving, and investing, you can take control of your financial future. The most important step is to begin, stay consistent, and adapt as you learn. Your journey to financial confidence starts with a single action.

Overcoming Money Myths and Building Financial Confidence

In a cozy cafe, the aroma of freshly brewed coffee fills the air as a young adult sits comfortably, engrossed in a financial advice blog on their tablet. The soft chatter of patrons and the clinking of cups create a soothing backdrop while they explore the intricacies of personal finance, eager to simplify the complexities that have long felt overwhelming. While scrolling through the blog, they come across several common misconceptions about money management that often hold people back from taking control of their financial futures.

The first misconception is the belief that **"you need a lot of money to start investing,"** a notion that has discouraged many from entering the investment world, assuming that substantial capital is a must. However, the rise of micro-investment platforms and fractional shares has changed the game, making it accessible to individuals with different financial backgrounds. Platforms like *Robinhood* and *Acorns* allow users to start investing with as little as $5, enabling them to buy fractional shares of high-value stocks. This means that even with a modest initial investment, one can own a piece of companies like *Apple* or *Amazon*, participating in the growth of these industry leaders. Regularly investing small amounts helps individuals harness the power of **compound interest**, gradually building a diversified portfolio over time.

Next, the young adult reads about the misconception that **"budgeting is restrictive and complicated,"** a belief that often stems from the idea that it involves tedious calculations and significant sacrifices. Budgeting is actually a tool for financial empowerment, providing a clear overview of income and expenses that enables informed spending decisions. One straightforward and effective method is the **50/30/20 rule**, which allocates:

- 50% of income for essential needs
- 30% for discretionary wants
- 20% for savings and debt repayment

This simple approach helps maintain a balanced financial life, ensuring that necessary expenses are covered while still allowing for personal spending and savings. Implementing such a method empowers individuals to take control of their finances without feeling deprived.

The third misconception addressed is the idea that **"debt is always bad."** While excessive debt can be harmful, not all debt is inherently negative. Understanding the difference between good debt and bad debt is crucial for effective financial management. Good debt, such as student loans or mortgages, represents an investment in one's future, often leading to increased earning potential or asset accumulation. These types typically carry lower interest rates and can yield long-term benefits, whereas bad debt, like high-interest credit card balances, can quickly escalate, resulting in financial strain. Recognizing these distinctions allows individuals to make strategic decisions that align with their financial goals.

Finally, the young adult encounters the misconception that **"financial advisors are only for the wealthy,"** a belief challenged by the rise of digital financial advisory services and robo- advisors, which offer affordable and accessible guidance to a broader audience. These platforms use algorithms to provide personalized investment advice and portfolio management, often at a fraction of the cost of traditional advisors. Services like *Betterment* and *Wealthfront* enable users to set financial goals and receive tailored recommendations, making professional advice attainable for those starting with limited capital.

As they continue to explore these insights, stories of individuals who have successfully navigated these misconceptions and taken control of their finances come to light. One story highlights a college graduate who, despite carrying student loans, began investing small amounts through a micro-investment app and, over time, built a diverse portfolio that contributed to their financial growth. Another features a young professional who, initially intimidated by the concept of budgeting, adopted the **50/30/20 rule** and discovered newfound freedom in managing expenses. These stories serve as powerful reminders that financial confidence is achievable for anyone willing to challenge common myths and embrace practical strategies.

The young adult, eager to boost their understanding of personal finance, logs into a virtual financial literacy workshop alongside a diverse group focused on enhancing their financial knowledge and skills. The facilitator, a seasoned financial advisor with over a decade of experience in wealth management, highlights the importance of continuous learning and clarifies that financial education is an ongoing journey rather than a one-time event. Resources like **books**, **podcasts**, and **online courses** are essential tools that provide varied perspectives and insights into effective money management. Regular engagement with these materials keeps participants informed about the latest financial trends, investment strategies, and budgeting techniques, equipping them to make informed decisions.

The concept of **"small wins"** in personal finance is introduced, which involves setting and achieving specific, measurable financial goals that build confidence by providing clear evidence of progress. For instance, a young adult might start by carefully tracking daily expenses using a detailed spreadsheet or a budgeting app that categorizes spending, enhancing awareness of habits while pinpointing areas for adjustments to boost savings. Another small win could be opening a high-yield savings account with automatic monthly deposits, ensuring consistent contributions to financial goals without the need for ongoing manual effort.

Recognizing and celebrating these small victories is vital for maintaining motivation and fostering confidence over time. Each achievement, no matter how small, reinforces the belief that financial goals are within reach. This positive reinforcement encourages individuals to set and pursue more ambitious objectives, gradually improving their financial literacy and resilience. The psychological benefits of acknowledging small wins are significant, helping to alleviate feelings of overwhelm and self-doubt that often accompany financial management.

Community support and accountability act as powerful motivators in the quest for financial confidence. The young adult finds reassurance in the workshop's supportive environment, where participants openly share experiences, challenges, and successes. This sense of camaraderie fosters a collective commitment to financial growth, as individuals hold each other accountable for their goals and progress. The facilitator encourages the formation of accountability partnerships, allowing participants to regularly check in with one another, share updates, and offer mutual encouragement. This support system enhances motivation and creates a valuable network for sharing resources and advice.

As the workshop progresses, the young adult feels increasingly empowered by the knowledge and support gained, starting to view financial management not as an overwhelming task but as a valuable opportunity for growth and self-improvement. The realization that financial confidence is attainable, regardless of initial capital, serves as a strong motivator. Armed with practical strategies and a supportive community, they are ready to take actionable steps toward their financial goals. The workshop concludes with a reminder that achieving financial success requires sustained effort and that each small win brings participants closer to their ultimate objectives. As they log off, the young adult feels a renewed sense of purpose and determination, eager to continue advancing toward financial independence.

In the quiet of their room, the young adult stands before a large corkboard, pinning images and notes that represent specific financial goals and aspirations. These items serve as tangible reminders of objectives, from saving **$5,000** for a dream vacation to accumulating **$100,000** for a solid retirement fund. Each image and note signifies a measurable step toward financial independence, acting as a visual roadmap that keeps them motivated and focused on their targets.

One effective strategy learned is the **"pay yourself first"** approach, which prioritizes savings by automatically setting aside a predetermined percentage of income—like **10%**—for savings before tackling other expenses. Treating savings as a fixed expense, similar to rent or utilities, ensures consistent contributions to financial goals. For example, setting up an automatic transfer of **10%** of each paycheck into a high-yield savings account can gradually build a substantial nest egg over time. This strategy encourages disciplined saving habits and reduces the chances of impulsive spending.

Building an emergency fund is another essential part of financial security, acting as a buffer that provides stability during unexpected expenses like medical emergencies or car repairs. Starting small is key; even setting aside **$20** per week can add up to over **$1,000** in a year. The ultimate goal is to save enough to cover three to six months' worth of essential living expenses. High-yield savings accounts, which typically offer interest rates significantly higher than traditional savings accounts, help the fund grow more efficiently over time.

Diversifying income streams enhances financial resilience. Engaging in side hustles or gig economy opportunities can provide additional income, reducing reliance on a single source. The digital landscape offers numerous possibilities, including:

- Freelance writing
- Graphic design
- Online tutoring
- Selling handmade crafts

Leveraging existing skills or acquiring new ones enables the creation of multiple income streams that contribute to financial stability and speed up progress toward objectives.

For those with variable income, such as freelancers or gig workers, managing finances can be particularly challenging. Budgeting based on average earnings rather than fluctuating monthly income provides a more stable foundation. This process involves calculating the average monthly income over the past six to twelve months and using this figure to create a realistic budget. Planning for lean months and saving during more prosperous periods helps maintain financial stability despite income variability.

Digital tools play a crucial role in simplifying these strategies. Budgeting apps like *Mint* and *YNAB* offer features that help track income and expenses, set specific savings goals, and monitor progress. These tools provide real-time insights into financial health, enabling informed decisions and adjustments as needed. Investment platforms like *Robinhood* and *Acorns* allow users to start investing with minimal capital, while financial planning software like *Quicken* or *Personal Capital* integrates budgeting, investment tracking, and retirement planning into one comprehensive interface.

Now more confident in their financial management skills, the young adult utilizes these digital tools to streamline strategies. Automating savings, meticulously tracking expenses, and actively exploring new income opportunities are proactive steps taken toward achieving financial goals. The process is ongoing, and as they continue to learn and adapt, they remain committed to building a secure and prosperous financial future.

Sitting on a park bench, the young adult gazes at the vibrant autumn leaves with a journal open on their lap. The tranquility of the park contrasts with a whirlwind of thoughts about their financial situation. As they jot down reflections, the idea of a **growth mindset** stands out, encouraging them to view personal finance challenges as opportunities for learning and improvement rather than insurmountable obstacles. This perspective helps individuals turn setbacks into actionable insights, fostering resilience and adaptability.

To nurture this mindset, it's crucial to reframe failures as learning experiences. Missing a savings goal shouldn't feel like a defeat; instead, it's a chance to analyze spending habits and refine financial strategies. Seeking feedback from trusted mentors or financial advisors can provide valuable insights, offering alternative perspectives and solutions. This proactive approach encourages continuous learning and adaptation, essential for successfully navigating the ever- changing financial landscape.

Facing financial challenges head-on is another key aspect of a growth mindset. Engaging in negotiations for bills or seeking better interest rates are practical steps that can lead to significant savings. For instance, a simple phone call to a service provider might result in a lower monthly bill or the removal of a fee, while exploring refinancing options for loans at lower interest rates can reduce monthly payments and create substantial savings over time. These actions require initiative and confidence, qualities that grow with each successful negotiation.

Setting long-term financial goals is vital for maintaining focus and motivation, as these objectives provide a guiding framework for decision-making and actions. Whether saving for a down payment on a house or building a retirement fund, having specific aims gives direction and purpose. However, it's equally important to stay adaptable to changing circumstances, as life's unpredictability means financial plans must be flexible enough to handle unexpected events, like job loss or medical emergencies. Regularly reviewing and adjusting goals ensures they remain relevant and achievable.

Persistence and resilience are key in the journey toward financial independence, as the path is rarely straightforward and often filled with setbacks and detours. Yet, each challenge overcome strengthens resolve and builds confidence. The young adult, reflecting on their progress, realizes that every small victory contributes to a larger story of growth and empowerment, fueling their determination to keep striving for financial freedom.

As the sun begins to set, casting a warm glow over the park, the young adult closes their journal, feeling a renewed sense of purpose. Yet, a lingering question remains: what lies ahead in their financial pursuits? The path to independence is filled with uncertainty, and the stakes are high. Just as they rise to leave, a notification buzzes on their phone—a reminder of an upcoming meeting with a potential business partner. The opportunity is promising, but the risks are significant, prompting the young adult to pause and consider the decision that could greatly impact their financial trajectory.

In this moment of suspense, the weight of the unknown feels heavy, as the choice to seize the opportunity or exercise caution hangs in the balance, placing the young adult at a critical juncture. The outcome is uncertain, and the implications are profound. As they walk away from the park, the air is thick with anticipation, the future a complex puzzle waiting to be solved. The pursuit continues, and the next chapter promises new challenges, insights, and revelations. What will they uncover in their quest for *financial independence*? The answer lies just beyond the horizon, waiting to be discovered.

Key Takeaway

You don't need a lot of money or a finance degree to start managing your money confidently. By embracing digital tools, setting small achievable goals, and adopting a growth mindset, anyone can build financial security from zero. Consistent small actions—like automating savings, tracking expenses, and learning from setbacks—are the real drivers of long-term financial success.

Chapter 2: Foundations of Financial Literacy

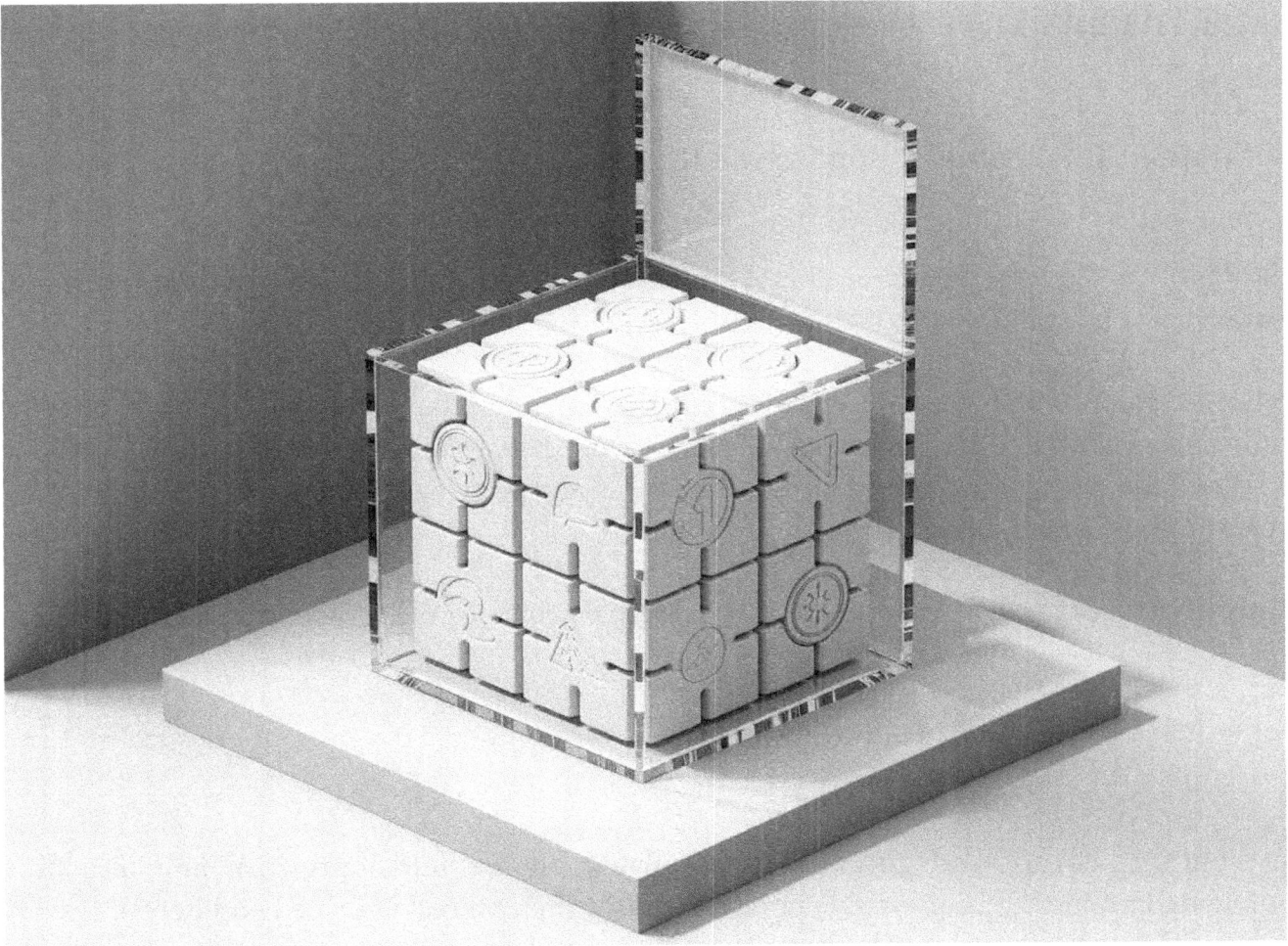

In a quiet corner of a local library, a young adult sits surrounded by stacks of financial books, a notebook open and pen in hand, creating an atmosphere of focused determination as they dive into the world of financial terminology and concepts, eager to build a solid foundation for their financial literacy. Mastering these terms is essential, as they form the basic language of finance, empowering individuals to make informed decisions and effectively navigate the complexities of money management.

The first set of terms to understand includes **assets**, **liabilities**, **equity**, and **net worth**.

- **Assets** are resources owned by an individual that have economic value, such as cash, real estate, stocks, and personal property.

- **Liabilities** are obligations or debts owed to others, including loans, credit card balances, and mortgages.
- **Equity** represents the ownership value in an asset after deducting liabilities. For example, if you own a house valued at $300,000 and owe $200,000 on the mortgage, your equity in the house is $100,000.
- **Net worth** is the difference between total assets and total liabilities, providing a snapshot of an individual's financial health. To calculate net worth, simply sum all assets and subtract all liabilities:

$$\text{Net Worth} = \text{Total Assets} - \text{Total Liabilities}$$

This figure serves as a key indicator of financial progress and stability, guiding decisions on spending, saving, and investing.

Next, the young adult focuses on **interest rates**, a fundamental concept in finance that significantly impacts both savings and loans. **Interest** represents the cost of borrowing money or the reward for saving it, expressed as a percentage of the principal amount. There are two primary types: simple and compound.

- **Simple interest** is calculated solely on the original principal, using the formula:

$$\text{Simple Interest} = \text{Principal} \times \text{Rate} \times \text{Time}$$

- In contrast, **compound interest** is calculated on the initial principal and also on the accumulated interest from previous periods, meaning that interest is earned on interest, leading to exponential growth over time. The formula for compound interest is:

$$A = P \left(1 + \frac{r}{n}\right)^{nt}$$

where A is the total amount of money accumulated after n years, including interest, P is the principal amount, r is the annual interest rate, n is the number of times that interest is compounded per year, and t is the time in years. Understanding the distinction between these two types is crucial, as compound interest can significantly enhance savings over time while also increasing the cost of loans if not managed wisely.

The young adult then examines **inflation**, which refers to the rate at which the general level of prices for goods and services rises, thereby eroding purchasing power. Over time, money loses value, resulting in the same amount purchasing fewer goods and services. For instance, if the inflation rate is 3% per year, a product that costs $100 today will cost $103 the following year. To preserve purchasing power, investing in assets that yield returns exceeding the inflation rate is essential. This may include stocks, real estate, or other investments that historically outperform inflation, ensuring that savings grow in real terms.

Credit scores and **reports** are another critical area of focus. A **credit score** is a numerical representation of an individual's creditworthiness, derived from their credit history, and it ranges from 300 to 850, with higher scores indicating better creditworthiness. Factors influencing scores include payment history, amounts owed, length of credit history, new credit, and types of credit utilized. A good score facilitates access to favorable borrowing terms, such as lower interest rates on loans and credit cards, while a poor score can limit financial opportunities. A **credit report** is a comprehensive record of an individual's credit history, encompassing information on credit accounts, payment history, and inquiries. Regularly reviewing reports is vital for identifying errors or fraudulent activity, ensuring that scores accurately reflect financial behavior.

As the young adult continues to take notes, they begin to recognize how these concepts interconnect, forming the backbone of financial literacy. Understanding these terms involves applying them to real-world situations to make informed financial decisions. For instance, grasping the impact of compound interest can motivate consistent saving, while awareness of inflation can guide investment choices. Recognizing the importance of a good credit score can lead to responsible credit management, unlocking opportunities for financial growth. With each page turned and note taken, the young adult builds a toolkit of knowledge that will serve as a foundation for their financial education.

In the midst of a lively financial debate club meeting, a young adult engages in spirited discussions about various financial scenarios and solutions, fostering critical thinking skills by encouraging participants to question assumptions, analyze quantitative data, and evaluate multiple perspectives. The club acts as a small-scale representation of the financial world, where decisions often exist in shades of gray, and the ability to think critically can greatly influence the achievement of financial goals.

One key lesson highlights the importance of scrutinizing financial advice, as accepting it without careful examination can lead to negative outcomes in a landscape filled with often contradictory information. The young adult approaches recommendations with a critical mindset, asking questions like:

1. What is the source of this advice?

2. What assumptions are behind it?
3. Are there any potential conflicts of interest that could affect the guidance?

Developing the habit of questioning helps them become more adept at distinguishing between reliable advice and misleading information.

Independent research emerges as another essential skill emphasized in the debate club, where the young adult delves into financial topics while seeking diverse sources of information to build a well-rounded understanding. This process involves critically evaluating news and data, identifying biases, and recognizing credible sources. For example, when analyzing an article about a new investment opportunity, they assess the publication's credibility, the author's qualifications, and any potential biases that could influence the narrative, empowering them to make informed decisions based on facts rather than opinions or sensationalism.

Skepticism plays a crucial role in avoiding scams and unrealistic offers, as the young adult examines case studies of common financial frauds, such as Ponzi schemes and phishing scams, to understand their mechanisms and identify warning signs. They learn to be wary of promises of guaranteed high returns with minimal risk, which often indicate fraudulent schemes. Maintaining a **skeptical** mindset helps them protect against financial predators and make decisions that align with their long-term goals.

Analytical thinking is further refined through activities like comparing financial products or evaluating investment options, where the young adult participates in exercises that involve assessing the pros and cons of various offerings, including credit cards, loans, or investment accounts. They consider critical factors such as interest rates, fees, and terms, as well as how these elements align with their objectives, deepening their understanding of products and enhancing their ability to make strategic choices.

Peer discussions and mentorship are vital in cultivating critical thinking skills, as the young adult benefits from the diverse perspectives and experiences of peers, who provide insights and challenge preconceived notions. Engaging in discussions with others navigating the complexities of finance creates a collaborative environment for learning and growth, while mentorship from more experienced individuals offers guidance and encouragement, helping them refine their analytical skills and build confidence in their decision-making abilities.

The young adult finds themselves in a lively community center, surrounded by peers eager to learn how to apply **financial literacy** to real-life situations. The workshop facilitator, an experienced financial advisor, kicks off the session with relatable scenarios that require thoughtful decision-making. The first example involves buying a car, a significant investment many young adults face. The facilitator highlights the importance of understanding the **total cost of ownership**, which includes not just the purchase price but also ongoing expenses like:

- insurance premiums
- routine maintenance
- fuel costs
- depreciation over time

They introduce the idea of comparing financing options, such as traditional loans versus leasing agreements, and stress the need to calculate the **annual percentage rate (APR)** to accurately assess the true cost of borrowing.

Next, the discussion shifts to renting an apartment, where the facilitator explains the necessity of budgeting for upfront costs, including security deposits and application fees, as well as ongoing expenses like:

- monthly rent
- utility bills
- renters insurance premiums

They emphasize evaluating the **opportunity cost** of renting versus buying a home, considering factors like current market conditions, personal financial stability, and long-term goals. The young adult learns to use a *rent-versus-buy calculator*, a helpful digital tool that simulates various scenarios to aid in informed decision-making.

Planning a vacation is another scenario explored, where the facilitator outlines steps to create a realistic budget that covers travel expenses, accommodation costs, meals, and recreational activities. They introduce the idea of setting a savings goal and using a *high-yield savings account* to build funds over time, encouraging the young adult to consider the opportunity cost of spending on a vacation versus the potential benefits of saving or investing that money for future financial goals.

The workshop then dives into budgeting for major life events, such as weddings, education, or starting a family. Detailed examples are provided, like creating a wedding budget that includes:

- venue rental
- catering services
- attire
- entertainment

They also discuss cost-saving measures like scheduling the event during off-peak times or opting for DIY decorations. For education, the importance of researching available scholarships, grants, and student loan options is discussed, along with calculating the **return on investment (ROI)** associated with different educational paths. When it comes to starting a family, the facilitator highlights the need to plan for:

- medical expenses
- childcare costs
- potential loss of income

They emphasize the critical importance of building an emergency fund.

The concept of opportunity cost is further examined through choices like saving versus investing, as the young adult learns to weigh the potential returns of investing in stocks or mutual funds against the security of a traditional savings account, considering factors such as risk tolerance and investment time horizon. Digital simulation tools are introduced, allowing participants to practice financial decision-making in a risk-free environment, providing a safe space to explore different strategies and their potential outcomes.

Throughout the workshop, the facilitator emphasizes the importance of adaptability and flexibility in financial planning, presenting case studies of unexpected life changes, such as job loss or medical emergencies, and discussing strategies for adjusting financial plans to accommodate these events. The young adult is encouraged to regularly review and update their financial goals and strategies, ensuring they remain aligned with changing circumstances.

As the session comes to a close, the young adult feels empowered, equipped with practical tools and strategies to navigate the complexities of financial decision-making. Yet, as they gather their belongings, a lingering question remains: how will they apply these lessons to their own life, where the stakes are real and the outcomes uncertain? Just as they prepare to leave, a notification buzzes on their phone—a message from a friend about a sudden opportunity to invest in a promising startup. The potential for significant returns is enticing, but the associated risks are equally daunting, leaving the young adult at a crossroads, the weight of the decision pressing heavily on their shoulders. The path forward is filled with uncertainty, and the choices they make now could significantly impact their financial future in ways they cannot yet predict. As they step out into the evening air, the tension is palpable, the future a vast expanse of possibilities waiting to be explored. What will they discover in their pursuit of financial independence? The answer lies just ahead, waiting to be uncovered.

Essential Financial Concepts for Beginners

Tip

Start your financial journey by leveraging digital tools that simplify budgeting, investing, and goal tracking. Apps like Mint, Acorns, or Robinhood allow you to manage money, invest small amounts, and monitor your progress—all from your phone. Begin with small, consistent steps: automate savings, track expenses, and set clear goals. These habits, supported by technology, build a strong foundation for financial confidence and long-term growth.

In the warm ambiance of a cozy café, a young adult sits comfortably, sipping a steaming cup of coffee while their tablet displays a series of financial podcasts and videos. The soft hum of conversation and the clinking of cups create a soothing backdrop as they explore financial concepts, eager to unravel the complexities that often seem daunting. This setting provides an ideal environment to examine key ideas essential for anyone starting to develop **financial literacy** and independence.

The exploration begins with **financial independence**, a term often used interchangeably with **financial freedom**, yet distinct in its implications. It refers to the state where an individual has accumulated enough personal wealth to cover basic living expenses without relying on active employment. This occurs when passive income from investments, savings, or other sources consistently meets or exceeds monthly expenses. In contrast, financial freedom encompasses a broader scope, including the ability to make life choices without being constrained by financial limitations. Achieving independence is a significant milestone on the path to freedom, implying greater control over one's financial life and allowing for choices that align with personal values and long-term aspirations.

A fundamental principle underpinning this independence is the **time value of money**, which highlights how money available today is worth more than the same amount in the future due to its potential earning capacity. This concept is crucial for understanding investment strategies and financial planning. For instance, if you have $1,000 today and invest it at an annual interest rate of 5%, it will grow to approximately $1,050 in one year. This growth potential emphasizes the importance of starting savings and investments early, as the benefits of compounding can significantly enhance wealth over time. The formula for future value, which calculates how much an investment made today will be worth in the future, is given by:

$$FV = PV \times (1 + r)^n$$

where FV is the future value, PV is the present value, r is the interest rate, and n is the number of periods.

Diversification is another critical concept in financial management, serving as a strategy to reduce investment risk by spreading investments across various asset classes, such as stocks, bonds, and real estate. This approach can mitigate the impact of poor performance in any single investment. It resembles maintaining a balanced diet, where consuming a variety of foods ensures that nutritional needs are met without over-relying on any single source. For example, while stocks may offer high returns, they also come with higher volatility. Balancing them with bonds, which typically provide more stable returns, can create a more resilient investment portfolio. The key is to find the right mix that aligns with one's risk tolerance and specific financial goals.

Liquidity, or the ease with which an asset can be converted into cash without affecting its market price, is another essential aspect of financial planning. Liquid assets, such as cash or stocks, can be quickly sold or exchanged for goods and services, providing financial flexibility in times of need. In contrast, illiquid assets, like real estate or collectibles, may take longer to sell and may not fetch their full market value immediately. Understanding the liquidity of assets is crucial for maintaining financial stability, as it ensures that funds are readily available to meet unexpected expenses or capitalize on investment opportunities.

As the young adult continues to explore these concepts, they begin to see how each one interconnects, forming a comprehensive framework for effective money management. The realization that financial independence, the time value of money, diversification, and liquidity are not just abstract ideas but practical tools for building wealth and achieving financial goals is empowering. With each sip of coffee and each new insight gained, the young adult becomes more equipped to navigate the financial landscape, ready to apply these principles in their pursuit of growth and confidence. The process of learning is just beginning, and there is much more to uncover.

When the young adult logs into an online seminar, a seasoned financial advisor greets them and begins to simplify the complexities of various investment vehicles. The advisor's clear and engaging voice makes the intricate world of investments accessible and easy to grasp. The session starts with an exploration of **stocks**, which represent ownership shares in a company and are known for their potential to deliver high returns, with historical average annual returns around 7- 10% after inflation. However, stocks come with significant risks due to market volatility, which can lead to price fluctuations of 20% or more in a single year. Investing in stocks requires thorough research into company fundamentals, market conditions, and a readiness to accept the inherent ups and downs of the market.

The discussion then shifts to **bonds**, essentially loans made to corporations or governments, which are generally considered safer than stocks. They offer more predictable returns in the form of interest payments, typically ranging from 2% to 5% annually. However, fluctuations in interest rates can inversely affect their market value. The advisor emphasizes the importance of assessing the creditworthiness of the bond issuer, as this directly impacts the likelihood of receiving the promised interest payments and the return of principal at maturity.

Next, **mutual funds** and **exchange-traded funds (ETFs)** are introduced as investment vehicles that pool capital from multiple investors to purchase a diversified portfolio of stocks, bonds, or other assets. Mutual funds are actively managed by professional fund managers who make investment decisions based on research and market analysis, while ETFs typically track a specific index and are traded on stock exchanges like individual stocks, often with lower expense ratios. Both options provide diversification, which can help mitigate risk, but they also come with management fees that can range from 0.1% to over 2%, potentially impacting overall returns.

Real estate is another investment vehicle discussed, offering the potential for both income and capital appreciation. Investing in real estate can involve purchasing physical properties, which may require significant capital and ongoing management, or investing in *real estate investment trusts (REITs)*, allowing individuals to invest in a diversified portfolio of real estate assets without the need to manage properties directly. While it can provide a steady income stream, often yielding 4-8% annually, and serve as a hedge against inflation, it also involves risks such as market fluctuations and the complexities of property management.

The advisor then explains the concept of a **diversified portfolio**, highlighting how spreading investments across different asset classes can reduce risk and enhance returns over time. Diversification is crucial in helping cushion the impact of poor performance in any single investment. Holding a mix of stocks, bonds, real estate, and other assets allows investors to achieve a balance that aligns with their risk tolerance, which can be quantitatively assessed using tools like the *Sharpe ratio*, and their financial goals.

Asset allocation is a critical component of investment strategy, involving the distribution of investments across various asset classes to achieve specific financial objectives. The advisor stresses the importance of aligning this allocation with personal risk tolerance and time horizon. For instance, a young investor with a long time horizon might allocate 70-80% of their portfolio to stocks for growth potential, while someone nearing retirement might prioritize bonds and other income-generating assets, allocating 60-70% to preserve wealth.

To illustrate the practical application of these concepts, the advisor provides examples of how different investment vehicles can be used to achieve specific financial objectives, such as retirement planning. A mix of stocks and bonds can provide both growth and income, while real estate investments can offer additional income streams through rental yields. For wealth preservation, a more conservative approach with a higher allocation to bonds and real estate might be appropriate, potentially allocating 50% to bonds and 30% to real estate.

The seminar concludes with a call to action, encouraging participants to explore digital platforms that offer access to a variety of investment options. Platforms like *Robinhood* and *Acorns* enable individuals to start investing with as little as $5, making it possible to build a diversified portfolio over time. The young adult leaves the seminar with a newfound understanding of investment vehicles and a sense of empowerment, ready to take actionable steps in their financial planning. Reflecting on the insights gained, they feel eager to continue researching opportunities and apply these strategies to achieve their financial goals.

In the heart of a bustling city park, a young adult settles onto a bench, surrounded by the lively energy of people passing by. Engrossed in a live stream on their tablet, they watch a stock market analyst break down the latest trends. This vibrant setting serves as a perfect backdrop to delve into the complexities of **financial markets**, which are essential for facilitating trade and investment.

These organized systems enable buyers and sellers to exchange financial assets, such as stocks, bonds, and commodities. They play a crucial role in efficiently allocating resources, allowing companies to raise capital for growth while giving individuals the chance to invest in opportunities that match their financial goals. The two main categories are **stock exchanges** and **over-the-counter (OTC) markets**.

Stock exchanges, like the New York Stock Exchange (NYSE) and NASDAQ, act as centralized platforms for trading securities. They provide a transparent and regulated environment that ensures transactions are conducted fairly and efficiently, following established rules. On the other hand, **OTC markets** function as decentralized networks where trading happens directly between parties, often involving securities not listed on formal exchanges. While these markets offer more flexibility, they also come with increased risks due to less regulation and transparency.

Market indices and benchmarks, such as the S&P 500 and Dow Jones Industrial Average, serve as performance indicators. The S&P 500, which includes 500 of the largest publicly traded companies in the U.S., gives a broad view of the market's overall health. In contrast, the Dow Jones consists of 30 significant companies and is often used to gauge general economic sentiment. These indices help investors assess trends and make informed decisions by providing a comparative analysis of current performance against historical data.

Volatility, marked by rapid and significant price changes, is a key factor that influences investment decisions. Various elements can trigger it, including:

- The release of economic data
- Geopolitical events
- Shifts in investor sentiment

Historical examples, like the 2008 financial crisis, illustrate how volatility can lead to major fluctuations that negatively impact confidence and decision-making. Understanding this phenomenon is vital for effective risk management and for crafting strategies that align with individual risk tolerance levels.

Market psychology plays a significant role in price movements, with concepts like **bull** and **bear markets** reflecting the prevailing sentiment. A bull market is characterized by rising prices and widespread optimism, while a bear market indicates declining prices and pervasive pessimism. Numerous factors, including economic indicators, corporate earnings reports, and global events, can influence sentiment. Recognizing these psychological factors helps investors anticipate potential shifts and adjust their strategies accordingly.

Staying informed about trends and economic indicators is essential for making timely and well-informed investment decisions. Digital tools and resources, such as financial news apps, market analysis platforms, and economic calendars, provide real-time updates and insights. These tools empower investors to monitor developments, track key indicators like *GDP growth* and *unemployment rates*, and proactively respond to potential changes.

The young adult sits cross-legged on their bed, smartphone in hand, exploring the setup of a financial management app that promises to transform their approach to personal finance. They enter their monthly income and itemized expenses, and the app generates a clear overview of their financial situation, highlighting specific areas for improvement and potential growth opportunities.

Creating a budget is the first step in mastering personal finance, and the app suggests the **50/30/20 rule**. This structured approach allocates:

- 50% of net income to essential needs
- 30% to discretionary wants
- 20% to savings and debt repayment

This method ensures that necessary expenses like housing and utilities are covered while still allowing for leisure spending and savings contributions. The young adult categorizes each expense, from groceries to entertainment subscriptions, and notices how the app automatically tracks spending patterns, providing insights into their financial behaviors.

Tracking expenses is crucial for maintaining oversight of finances, and the app's expense tracking feature categorizes each transaction, offering a detailed view of spending habits. This transparency helps identify areas where they can cut back, freeing up funds for savings or debt repayment. Setting spending limits for each category allows the user to receive notifications when they approach their budgeted thresholds, encouraging more intentional spending practices.

Setting financial goals is another key element of personal finance management, and the app allows users to define both short-term and long-term objectives, such as saving for a vacation or building a retirement fund. Breaking these goals into actionable steps creates a structured plan for achieving them, complete with progress tracking and motivational reminders. The young adult sets a target to save **$5,000** for an emergency fund, which acts as a vital financial buffer for unexpected expenses.

Building an emergency fund is essential for financial stability, and the app supports this by facilitating automated transfers to a high-yield savings account, ensuring consistent contributions without manual effort. Starting with small, regular deposits, the young adult monitors their savings growth, fostering a sense of security and providing a cushion against financial disruptions.

Debt management is another important aspect of personal finance, and the app introduces the **snowball** and **avalanche methods**, two effective strategies for systematically reducing debt. The snowball method focuses on paying off the smallest debts first, leading to quick wins and increased motivation, while the avalanche method prioritizes debts with the highest interest rates, minimizing total interest paid over time. The young adult chooses the avalanche method, setting up automatic payments to tackle high-interest credit card debt.

Insurance is a critical part of financial planning, protecting against potential losses, and the app offers insights into various types of coverage, including health, life, and property insurance, and their importance in a well-rounded financial strategy. Evaluating options and associated costs helps the young adult make informed decisions about the protection they need.

Digital tools and apps are invaluable for optimizing personal finance management, and the app's features—budgeting, expense tracking, goal setting, and debt management—provide a solid toolkit for achieving financial confidence. The young adult explores these functionalities and feels empowered to take control of their financial journey.

As they close the app and set their phone aside, a notification catches their eye—a message from a friend about a sudden opportunity to invest in a promising startup. The potential for substantial returns is enticing, but the risks are significant, and the young adult finds themselves at a decision point, the weight of the choice pressing on their mind. The next steps are filled with uncertainty, and the decisions they make now could greatly impact their financial future in unpredictable ways. Sitting in the dim light of their room, the atmosphere is charged with anticipation, the future a wide array of possibilities waiting to be explored. What insights will they gain in their pursuit of financial independence? The answer lies just ahead, ready to be uncovered.

Chapter 3: Setting Realistic Financial Goals

The young adult sits at a minimalist desk, surrounded by sticky notes and a vision board, contemplating their financial future. The room is quiet, save for the soft rustle of paper as they jot down specific ideas and measurable aspirations, marking the starting point for establishing realistic financial goals that are essential for achieving independence and growth. The process begins with a clear understanding of **SMART** financial goals: **Specific, Measurable, Achievable, Relevant**, and **Time-bound**. These criteria provide a structured framework that turns vague aspirations into actionable plans, creating a clear strategy for success.

Specific goals eliminate ambiguity and ensure clarity in what you aim to achieve. For instance, instead of a general goal like *"save money,"* a specific goal would be *"save $5,000 for an emergency fund."* **Measurable** goals allow you to track your progress and maintain motivation.

In this case, you can measure your progress by the amount saved each month, such as aiming to save *$417* monthly to reach your target within a year. **Achievable** goals are realistic and attainable, considering your current financial situation and available resources; thus, saving *$5,000* in a year might be feasible if you can allocate *$417* monthly. **Relevant** goals align with broader life objectives and values, ensuring that your financial plans support your overall vision. Finally, **time-bound** goals have a clear deadline, providing a sense of urgency and focus; setting a one-year timeframe for your emergency fund goal creates a specific endpoint to work toward.

Prioritizing financial goals involves balancing immediate needs with long-term aspirations. A tiered system can help categorize them into:

- Short-term objectives (e.g., building an emergency fund, paying off high-interest debt)
- Medium-term objectives (e.g., saving for a vacation, purchasing a new car)
- Long-term objectives (e.g., retirement planning, buying a home)

This approach ensures that urgent needs are met while still progressing toward future aspirations.

Short-term goals serve as foundational steps toward larger financial objectives. For example, saving for a vacation can teach discipline and budgeting skills, which are essential for more significant goals like homeownership, while building an emergency fund provides a financial safety net, reducing stress and allowing you to concentrate on long-term planning. These smaller goals build momentum and confidence, reinforcing the habit of setting and achieving targets.

Aligning financial goals with personal values and lifestyle is crucial for maintaining motivation and ensuring that each goal supports your overall life vision. If travel and experiences are important, allocating funds for vacations aligns with your values and enhances your quality of life. Conversely, if security and stability are priorities, focusing on debt repayment and savings might take precedence. This alignment ensures that financial goals are not just numbers on a page but meaningful steps toward a fulfilling life.

Digital tools and apps play a vital role in setting and tracking financial goals. Many offer goal- setting templates, progress tracking, and motivational reminders, making it easier to stay on track. For instance, apps like *Mint* or *YNAB* allow you to set specific savings goals, monitor progress, and receive alerts when nearing your target. These tools provide a visual representation of your financial journey, offering encouragement and accountability.

Breaking down large financial goals into manageable action steps is essential for maintaining focus and motivation. Consider saving for a down payment on a home; this large goal can be daunting, but breaking it into smaller steps makes it more achievable. Start by determining the total amount needed for the down payment, then calculate how much to save monthly to reach that goal within your desired timeframe. Set up automatic transfers to a dedicated savings account, and regularly review your progress to stay motivated.

Regular reviews and adjustments are necessary to accommodate changing circumstances or priorities. Life is unpredictable, and financial plans must be flexible to adapt to new situations. Reviewing your goals regularly allows for necessary adjustments, ensuring that your plans remain relevant and achievable. This practice also provides an opportunity to celebrate progress and reassess priorities, keeping your strategy aligned with your evolving life vision.

Achieving financial goals offers significant psychological benefits, such as increased confidence and reduced financial stress. Each accomplished goal reinforces your ability to manage money effectively, boosting self-esteem and motivation. This positive reinforcement encourages continued commitment to financial plans, creating a cycle of success and growth. Each achievement enhances overall well-being, motivating you to pursue even greater aspirations.

Chapter 4: Tracking Your Money

Tip

Start simple: If you're new to money tracking, choose a digital app with automatic categorization and bank sync. This saves time, reduces manual errors, and helps you quickly spot spending patterns. As you get comfortable, customize categories to fit your lifestyle. Remember, consistency is more important than perfection—review your finances weekly to stay on track and build lasting habits.

The young adult, driven by specific financial goals, sits at a desk cluttered with bank statements and receipts, while a laptop displays a financial dashboard that brightens the dimly lit room. This marks the beginning of an important journey toward financial independence: creating a comprehensive money tracking system. Understanding where every dollar comes from and where it goes is essential for gaining financial control. Being aware of spending habits and income sources is crucial for making informed decisions and achieving goals.

The first step is to choose a tracking method that fits personal preferences and lifestyle. There are several options available, each with its own pros and cons:

- **Digital applications**: Popular for their convenience and automation features, often including automatic expense categorization, bank synchronization, and detailed spending reports. Apps like *Mint* or *YNAB* (You Need A Budget) can connect directly to bank accounts, providing real-time updates and insights into financial behavior. However, users should feel comfortable with technology and be aware of data privacy considerations.

- **Spreadsheets**: Offer a more customizable approach, as software like *Microsoft Excel* or *Google Sheets* allows users to create personalized systems tailored to their specific needs. This method provides flexibility in categorizing expenses and income but requires manual data entry and a basic understanding of spreadsheet functions. It's particularly suitable for those who prefer a hands-on approach and have the time to keep their records updated.

- **Traditional pen-and-paper systems**: The simplest but also the most labor-intensive, as recording every transaction by hand can be time-consuming. Yet, this method fosters a tangible connection to one's finances. It works best for those who enjoy a tactile experience and have the discipline to consistently update their records.

Once a method is chosen, the next step is to categorize expenses, which is vital for analyzing spending patterns and identifying areas for improvement. Common categories include:

- **Housing**
- **Utilities**
- **Groceries**
- **Entertainment**
- **Savings**

Each category should accurately reflect the individual's lifestyle and financial priorities. For example, someone who values travel might set aside a separate category for vacation expenses. Categorizing helps in establishing realistic budgets and tracking progress toward goals.

Tracking all sources of income is equally important, including the primary salary, side jobs, and passive income streams like dividends or rental income. Having a complete view of income sources is essential for accurate budgeting and financial planning, ensuring that all potential resources are accounted for and effectively utilized.

Digital tools and applications can significantly simplify the tracking process, as many offer features like automatic expense categorization that save time and reduce the risk of errors. Bank synchronization allows for seamless integration of financial data, providing a comprehensive view of one's situation, while spending reports offer insights into behavior, highlighting areas where adjustments may be needed.

Setting up a digital money tracking app involves a few straightforward steps:

1. Download and install the chosen app.
2. Input financial data, including income and expenses, which may involve linking bank accounts for automatic updates or manually entering transactions.
3. Customize categories to reflect personal spending habits, which is crucial for accurate tracking.
4. Regularly update and review the system to maintain control. Dedicating time each week to enter transactions and analyze spending patterns is key to staying on track with goals.

Visualizing spending patterns can have a powerful psychological effect, increasing awareness of financial behavior and motivating individuals to make necessary changes. For instance, realizing that a large portion of income is spent on dining out may inspire someone to cook more meals at home, freeing up funds for savings or other priorities. The visual representation of financial data can be a strong tool for fostering discipline and encouraging positive changes in spending habits. As the young adult continues to refine their tracking system, they start to see the tangible benefits of this increased awareness.

As the young adult reviews their financial dashboard, a clear pattern emerges from the detailed graphs and charts, showing a consistent overspend in the **dining out** category over the past month. This often represents 20-30% of discretionary income for many individuals. Recognizing this trend highlights the importance of analyzing spending habits to identify specific areas for improvement and potential savings. A thorough examination of these patterns enables data-driven decisions that support measurable financial growth.

Monthly spending reports become vital, as each line item offers valuable insights. The young adult learns to interpret the data, spotting both obvious overspending and subtle, unexpected expenses that can add up unnoticed. These might include:

- Impulse purchases averaging $50 per month
- Forgotten subscriptions costing $10 to $15 each

Together, these can deplete resources. By comparing actual spending against budgeted amounts, they gain a clearer understanding of their financial health, allowing for informed adjustments to future budgets.

Aligning expenditures with budgeted amounts requires careful attention to detail. Setting realistic spending limits—like capping dining out expenses at **$150** per month—and sticking to them can help reduce the risks associated with financial mismanagement. This approach emphasizes not just cutting costs but also making strategic choices that align with specific financial goals, such as saving for a down payment on a home.

Minimizing unnecessary expenses becomes a key focus as the young adult reviews subscription services, identifying those that no longer provide value, and opts to prepare *home-cooked meals* instead of dining out multiple times a week. They also look for cost-effective alternatives for recurring expenses, such as switching to a more affordable internet plan. Each decision helps redirect savings from reduced expenses toward achieving financial goals, reinforcing the link between diligent tracking, saving, and goal attainment.

Digital tools are essential in this process, offering insights and actionable suggestions for spending adjustments. Features like spending alerts, budget recommendations, and trend analysis become invaluable resources. These tools provide real-time feedback, alerting the user when they approach spending limits and offering tailored recommendations for maintaining budget discipline. The young adult sets up alerts within their tracking system, ensuring they receive notifications before exceeding budget thresholds, which encourages a proactive approach to financial management.

The long-term benefits of consistent money tracking and spending adjustments are substantial, as increased savings, reduced financial stress, and enhanced control are just the beginning. The young adult continues to refine their financial habits, gaining a newfound sense of empowerment and confidence, making the journey toward financial independence more manageable and their objectives clearer.

However, while reflecting on their progress, a notification pings on their phone—a message from a friend about a sudden market downturn, reminding them of the unpredictable nature of financial markets. A wave of uncertainty arises, realizing that despite careful planning, external factors can still present significant challenges. The question emerges: How will they tackle this new obstacle? The answer remains unclear, and the anticipation of what lies ahead creates a sense of urgency, motivating them to seek solutions to navigate this evolving financial landscape.

Creating a Simple, Personalized Budget

The young adult, feeling more confident after analyzing their spending habits, sits at a desk with a fresh notebook and a budgeting app open on their laptop, marking the start of an important phase in financial management: creating a clear, customized budget. Budgeting is not just about limiting spending; it serves as a strategic framework for success, outlining a clear pathway to achieving personal financial goals. **Personalization** is key, as each person's circumstances and aspirations vary widely. A well-structured budget captures these differences, ensuring it aligns with one's lifestyle and objectives.

The first step in creating a budget is calculating total monthly income, which involves a thorough assessment of all income sources beyond the primary salary. This should include:

- Side jobs
- Freelance work
- Passive income streams like dividends or rental income

This ensures that all potential resources are accounted for and establishes a solid foundation for planning. For example, if the primary salary is $3,000, a side job contributes $500, and passive income adds another $200, the total monthly income would be $3,700.

Next, itemizing fixed expenses is essential. These unavoidable costs remain constant each month, including:

- Rent
- Utilities
- Loan payments

Fixed expenses form the backbone of the budget, as they are necessary and predictable; for instance, if rent is $1,200, utilities average $150, and loan payments total $300, these would sum to $1,650. Understanding these figures is crucial for grasping the minimum monthly obligations.

After identifying fixed expenses, the focus shifts to variable costs, which include groceries, entertainment, and dining out that can change from month to month. Making realistic estimates based on past spending patterns is important, as reviewing previous months' expenses can provide a reliable baseline for these categories. For example, if groceries typically cost $400, entertainment $150, and dining out $100, these variable expenses would total $650, making it essential to be practical in these estimates for creating a budget that is both achievable and sustainable.

Allocating a portion of income for savings and financial goals is a critical part of budgeting, with a widely recommended guideline suggesting at least **20%** of income for savings. This percentage can be adjusted based on individual circumstances, but the focus should be on consistent saving; for instance, with a total income of $3,700, setting aside 20% would mean saving $740 each month, which can be directed towards an emergency fund, retirement accounts, or other objectives.

Establishing an emergency fund is vital for stability, serving as a cushion for unexpected expenses like medical emergencies or car repairs. A common guideline is to aim for an emergency fund that covers **3-6 months** of essential expenses; if monthly expenses total $2,300, it should ideally range between $6,900 and $13,800. Gradually building this fund by setting aside a portion of savings each month can enhance security and provide peace of mind.

Flexibility is an important aspect of budgeting, as life can be unpredictable. Budgets should adapt to accommodate changes such as income fluctuations or unexpected expenses. Regularly reviewing and adjusting the budget ensures it remains relevant and effective; for example, if income increases, it may be wise to allocate additional funds towards savings or debt repayment, while conversely, if an unexpected expense arises, temporarily reducing discretionary spending can help maintain financial balance.

Digital tools can significantly simplify the budgeting process, as numerous apps offer features like:

- Automatic expense tracking
- Budget templates
- Customizable alerts

These tools save time and reduce the risk of errors, making budgeting more accessible and manageable; for instance, setting up alerts for when spending approaches budget limits can help maintain discipline and prevent overspending.

Establishing both short-term and long-term financial goals is an integral part of budgeting. Short-term goals might include saving for a vacation or paying off a small debt, while long-term goals could involve retirement planning or purchasing a home. Incorporating these goals into the budget ensures steady progress towards achieving them; for example, if a short-term goal is to save $1,200 for a vacation in six months, allocating $200 each month can make this goal attainable.

Regular budget reviews are essential for maintaining financial discipline. A monthly assessment allows for evaluating progress, making necessary adjustments, and reinforcing positive habits. This practice keeps the budget aligned with current circumstances and provides an opportunity to acknowledge achievements and sustain motivation.

The psychological benefits of budgeting are significant, as it can boost financial confidence, reduce stress, and foster a greater sense of control over one's future. Knowing there is a structured plan for managing money can alleviate anxiety and empower individuals to make informed decisions.

The young adult continues to refine their budget, experiencing these benefits firsthand and gaining confidence and clarity in financial management.

Chapter 5: Digital Tools for Money Management

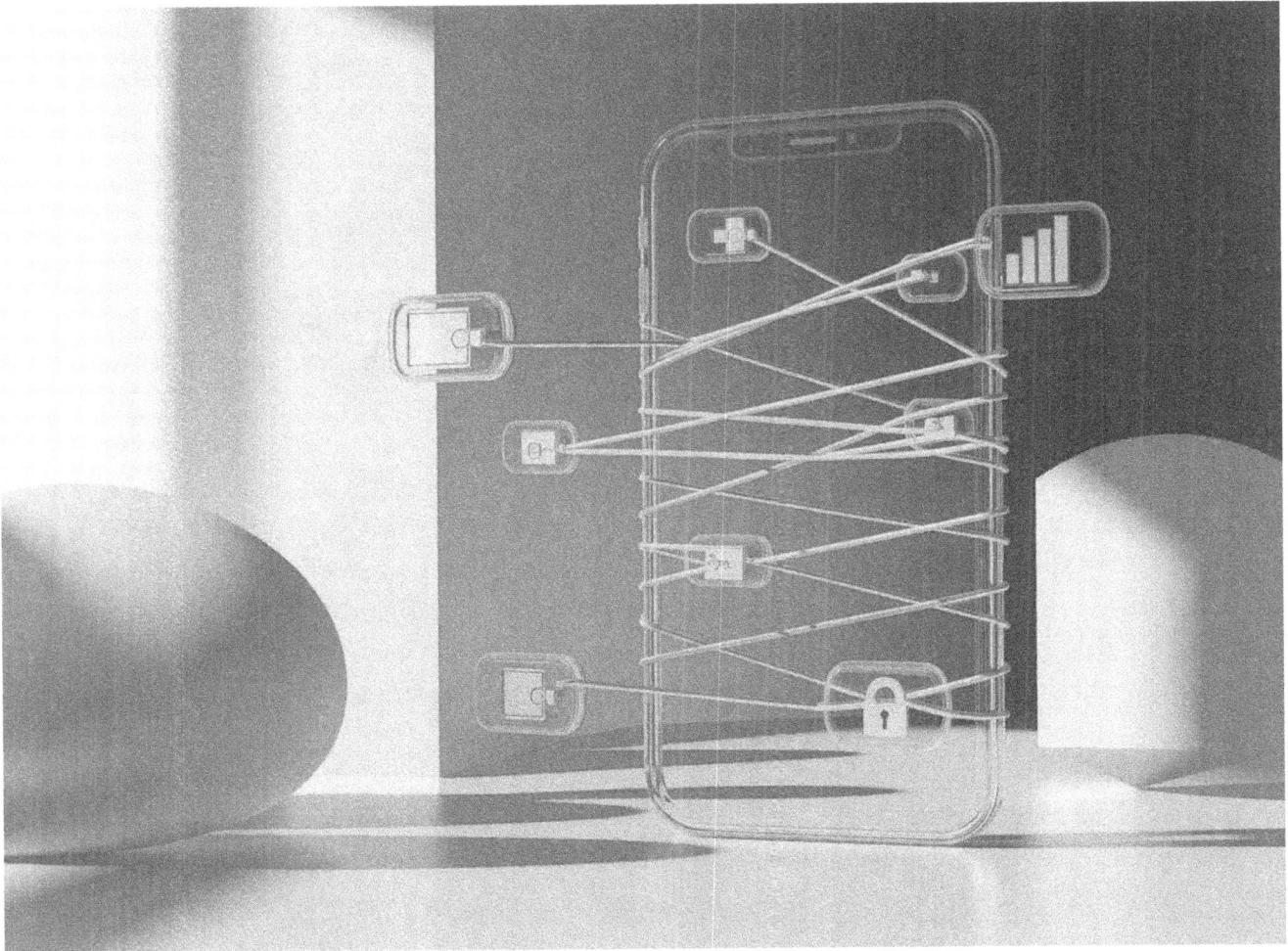

Tip

Start with one or two digital tools that match your current needs—like a budgeting app and an automated savings app. As you grow more comfortable, gradually add investment or planning platforms. This step-by-step approach prevents overwhelm and helps you build confidence while tracking your progress. Remember, consistency is key: check in with your chosen tools regularly to stay on top of your financial goals and adapt as your situation evolves.

The young adult, now more financially savvy, sits at their desk with a laptop open, showcasing a variety of digital tools designed to enhance money management skills. The glow from the screen reflects a newfound determination to use technology in the pursuit of **financial independence**. These tools have become essential for effective financial management, offering user-friendly interfaces that cater to both beginners and seasoned users. They represent a significant shift in how individuals can take charge of their financial futures.

Selecting the right tools is crucial, as each person's financial situation is unique and shaped by their specific needs and goals. The wide range of options available today allows for tailored solutions across different aspects of money management. For instance, personal finance apps like *Mint*, *YNAB* (You Need A Budget), and *PocketGuard* provide extensive features, including:

- budgeting
- expense tracking
- financial goal setting

These tools give users real-time insights into their spending habits, empowering them to make informed decisions and stay on track with their financial objectives.

Investment platforms such as *Robinhood* and *Acorns* are designed for beginners, offering educational resources and low entry barriers that make investing accessible for those with limited experience. They simplify the investment process, allowing users to start with small amounts and gradually build their portfolios. For example, *Robinhood* offers commission-free trades, while *Acorns* automates investments by rounding up purchases to the nearest dollar and investing the spare change, enabling users to begin without a large initial investment.

Automated savings apps like *Digit* and *Qapital* make saving easier by automating the process. They analyze spending patterns and automatically set aside small amounts for savings, creating a seamless experience. *Digit* uses algorithms to determine how much money can be safely saved without impacting daily expenses, while *Qapital* allows users to set specific savings goals and rules, such as rounding up purchases or saving a set amount when certain conditions are met.

Financial planning software like *Personal Capital* provides a comprehensive view of an individual's financial health, including net worth, investment performance, and retirement planning. By consolidating data from multiple accounts, it offers users a detailed snapshot of their financial situation. Visualizing their financial landscape helps them make more informed decisions about their future.

Robo-advisors, such as *Betterment* and *Wealthfront*, offer an accessible way to invest with low fees and personalized portfolio management. They use algorithms to create and manage portfolios based on individual risk tolerance and financial goals. The cost-effective structure and user- friendly design make them an attractive option for those new to investing.

For those interested in digital currencies, cryptocurrency platforms like *Coinbase* and *Binance* provide opportunities for investment. However, caution is key, as the market is highly volatile and requires thorough research and an understanding of the associated risks.

Online educational resources and communities, including financial blogs, podcasts, and forums, are invaluable for expanding knowledge and staying informed about trends and strategies. Engaging with these resources can provide insights and advice from experts and peers, deepening understanding of effective money management.

Data security and privacy are essential when using digital tools. Recommended practices include:

- using strong passwords
- enabling two-factor authentication
- regularly reviewing app permissions to protect personal information

Setting up financial alerts and notifications can help users monitor account activity, bill payments, and progress toward goals, reinforcing proactive money management habits.

Using digital tools offers psychological benefits, such as enhanced financial clarity and increased motivation through visual progress tracking. The empowerment that comes from taking control of one's financial situation can lead to greater confidence and a more secure future. The young adult continues to explore and integrate these tools into their routine, witnessing firsthand the transformative impact of technology on achieving financial growth and independence.

Choosing the Right Digital Financial Apps

The young adult sits at their desk, surrounded by various digital devices, each displaying different financial applications. The soft glow of the screens lights up the room, highlighting their focused expression. An open notepad is ready for notes, while a checklist titled **"Steps for Evaluating Financial Apps"** is prominently displayed on the laptop screen. This organized approach is essential for selecting the right app that fits their unique financial needs and personal lifestyle.

The first step on the checklist reads: **"Identify Your Financial Needs and Goals."** They start by writing down their personal financial objectives, which include:

- Creating a detailed budget for monthly expenses
- Saving a specific amount for a dream vacation
- Building a diversified investment portfolio aimed at securing a comfortable retirement

Each goal is specific, measurable, and aligned with their current lifestyle, providing a clear path for financial planning.

Next, the focus shifts to **"Research App Features and Reviews."** The young adult browses app stores, carefully reading user reviews and comparing features across multiple platforms. They pay close attention to the user interface, ease of navigation, and compatibility with their devices. A well-designed app should be intuitive and fit seamlessly into daily routines, making financial management easier rather than more complicated.

The checklist continues with **"Evaluate App Security and Privacy."** In a time when data breaches are a major concern, they thoroughly examine privacy policies, check for security certifications like *ISO 27001*, and ensure the app uses strong encryption protocols to protect personal data. This step is crucial, as safeguarding financial information is vital for maintaining trust and security.

"Consider Cost and Value" prompts them to analyze various pricing models, weighing the benefits of free versions against subscription fees or one-time purchases while calculating the total cost of ownership over time. The goal is to find an app that delivers the best value for money, offering essential features without unnecessary expenses. This analysis involves careful consideration of the app's benefits relative to its price to ensure a smart investment in their financial toolkit.

"Test Usability with Free Trials" appears next on the checklist. They download trial versions of promising apps, assessing functionality and intuitiveness while exploring how well these apps integrate with their existing financial accounts. This ensures a smooth transition and minimal disruption to their current financial setup.

The checklist includes **"Assess Customer Support and Resources."** The young adult reviews the availability of customer support options, such as live chat, email, or phone support, and evaluates response times. They also look for educational resources like video tutorials or comprehensive FAQs, which can be invaluable for troubleshooting and maximizing the app's potential.

"Look for Community Feedback" encourages them to participate in online forums and communities dedicated to personal finance. They seek opinions and experiences from other users who share similar financial goals to gain insights that might not be obvious from reviews alone. This step fosters a sense of community and shared learning, enhancing their understanding of the app's real-world performance.

Finally, the checklist concludes with **"Regularly Review and Adapt."** They set reminders to periodically reassess the app's effectiveness, ensuring it continues to meet their evolving financial needs and lifestyle changes. This proactive approach guarantees that financial management tools remain relevant and effective, adapting to new challenges and opportunities as they arise.

With the checklist complete, the young adult leans back, feeling accomplished after a thorough evaluation process. They have taken a significant step toward financial independence, equipped with the right digital tools to support their financial management. This methodical approach not only enhances their skills but also instills a sense of confidence and control over their financial future.

Comparing Banking, Budgeting, and Investment Apps

Tip

When choosing digital financial apps, always prioritize security features like two-factor authentication, end-to-end encryption, and regular security updates. Don't just focus on convenience—review each app's privacy policy and user feedback for any history of data breaches. Remember, a user-friendly interface is important, but protecting your financial data is essential for long-term confidence and peace of mind. Take time to compare security protocols before committing to any app.

The young adult, now more financially savvy, sits in front of a large digital whiteboard displayed on a monitor, carefully analyzing various financial apps organized into three distinct columns: **banking**, **budgeting**, and **investment**. Each column is filled with detailed notes and comparisons, reflecting a thorough examination of the functionalities and security measures of these digital tools.

In the banking apps column, the young adult reviews features essential for everyday financial management. **Real-time balance updates** stand out, giving users an immediate view of their financial standing, which is especially helpful for those needing to make quick decisions or closely monitor spending patterns. **Transaction history** is another key feature, providing a comprehensive record of all financial activities that aids in tracking expenses and spotting unauthorized transactions.

Mobile check deposit adds convenience by eliminating the need to visit a bank branch for depositing checks, streamlining the process for users who prefer managing their finances entirely online. **Bill payment options** are also examined, focusing on apps that offer automated payments and reminders to help users consistently meet their obligations without the risk of missing a due date.

Security is a top priority, and special attention is given to apps with strong features. **Two-factor authentication** is essential, providing an extra layer of security by requiring a second form of verification beyond just a password. **Biometric login**, such as fingerprint or facial recognition, is highly valued for its blend of security and convenience. Each app's user interface is assessed, noting how quickly and intuitively transactions can be navigated, with a preference for a simple and clean design that enhances the overall experience.

In the budgeting apps column, the focus shifts to features that support effective financial planning. **Automatic expense tracking** stands out, saving time and reducing the chances of human error in recording transactions. Apps that categorize expenses automatically are particularly useful, offering insights into spending patterns and helping users identify areas for cutting costs.

Budget forecasting tools are another critical feature, allowing users to project their future financial situation based on current spending habits, which is invaluable for setting realistic goals and planning for upcoming expenses. The importance of *data encryption* and *secure cloud storage* is highlighted to protect sensitive information from unauthorized access.

Ease of use is significant in the evaluation process, as different input methods for transactions, such as manual entry, voice commands, and receipt scanning, are tested to find which app provides the most seamless experience. **Dynamic charts and graphs** are also assessed, offering a visual representation of financial data that makes it easier to understand and analyze.

In the investment apps column, features catering to both novice and experienced investors are explored. **Stock tracking** is a fundamental feature, allowing users to monitor the performance of their investments in real-time. **Portfolio management tools** are crucial, providing a comprehensive view of all investments and helping users make informed decisions about buying, selling, or holding assets.

Educational resources are particularly important for novice investors, offering tutorials, articles, and videos that explain investment concepts and strategies in detail. Security features such as secure transaction protocols and account monitoring alerts are essential, ensuring that investments are protected against fraud and unauthorized access.

The app's usability is evaluated by simulating trades and exploring various investment options, with clarity and speed of transactions being key factors that directly impact the user experience and the ability to respond quickly to market changes. This ongoing assessment of features leads to a deeper understanding of how each app can support financial management, paving the way for further analysis and informed decision-making.

The young adult, now fully immersed in the intricacies of app security, examines a tablet showcasing a detailed comparison chart of security protocols used by banking, budgeting, and investment applications. This analysis is crucial, as protecting financial data is essential in today's digital world.

When looking at banking apps, the young adult highlights **end-to-end encryption**, a key security feature that ensures data is encrypted on the sender's device and only decrypted on the recipient's device, effectively blocking unauthorized access during transmission. They also assess compliance with data protection regulations like the *General Data Protection Regulation (GDPR)*. Although GDPR is a European regulation, many apps operating internationally, including those in the U.S., adopt it to maintain high data protection standards. Security certifications such as **ISO 27001** indicate that an app meets globally recognized benchmarks for information security management systems.

The young adult explores additional security layers, including **fraud detection algorithms** that use machine learning to identify unusual patterns that may signal fraudulent activity. **Secure APIs** (Application Programming Interfaces) facilitate safe communication between the app and external services, ensuring that data exchanges are protected from interception or tampering.

Shifting to budgeting apps, they analyze **data anonymization techniques** that enhance user privacy by removing personally identifiable information from data sets. This ensures that even if data is compromised, it cannot be traced back to an individual user. **Secure login procedures**, like **two-factor authentication**, are considered essential for preventing unauthorized access, as this method requires a second verification step, such as a code sent to a user's mobile device, in addition to the standard password.

The ability to manage data sharing with third-party applications is another important feature, allowing users to grant or revoke access to their data and ensuring they maintain control over who can view or use their information. User feedback is reviewed to identify common security concerns, such as data breaches or unauthorized data sharing, and how developers address these issues through software updates or improved security measures.

In the realm of investment apps, the importance of **SIPC** (Securities Investor Protection Corporation) insurance is emphasized, protecting investment accounts up to $500,000, including a $250,000 limit for cash claims, in the event of a brokerage failure. **Secure financial transaction protocols**, such as **Transport Layer Security (TLS)**, are vital for encrypting data during transactions, preventing interception by malicious actors.

Regular security audits involve independent assessments of an app's measures to uncover vulnerabilities and ensure compliance with industry standards. The availability of **multi-layer authentication options** boosts security by requiring multiple forms of verification before granting access to an account.

Transparency in security policy updates is essential, as it keeps users informed about changes to security measures and enables them to take necessary actions to protect their accounts. Apps that communicate clearly and frequently about security updates are more likely to build user trust.

As the young adult continues to analyze these protocols, they gain a deeper understanding of the measures needed to protect their financial data. This knowledge empowers them to make informed choices about which apps to use, ensuring their information remains secure while they pursue their financial goals.

The young adult, surrounded by friends, kicks off a detailed usability test with laptops and smartphones arranged on a table, each device showcasing a different financial app. The atmosphere is filled with excitement as they prepare to evaluate the functionality of various digital money management tools, and each participant is eager to share specific feedback based on their experiences.

As testing begins, the focus shifts to banking apps, where friends navigate through multiple interfaces and assess the responsiveness of customer service via chat support. They simulate common scenarios, such as disputing a transaction or asking about specific account features, carefully noting response times and the quality of assistance received. The young adult diligently documents feedback on app design, pinpointing which interfaces are **user-friendly** and which require a bit more effort to master. Ease of navigation is essential, as users prefer apps that allow them to complete tasks efficiently, ideally within three clicks, while ensuring clear pathways.

Next, the group explores budgeting apps, entering a range of expenses, from daily coffee purchases to monthly rent, while observing how each app accommodates different financial habits. The young adult tracks the speed at which the apps process data and how easily users can customize categories to reflect their unique spending patterns. Testers closely examine the visual representation of financial data, assessing how effectively charts and graphs illustrate spending trends and adherence to budgets. The ability to quickly identify areas of overspending or potential savings is crucial for a budgeting app's usability.

Investment apps are the final focus of the usability tests, where participants engage with simulated investment scenarios and utilize educational resources designed to clarify complex financial concepts. The young adult gathers feedback on the clarity of investment summaries, noting which apps provide concise, understandable overviews and which leave users feeling puzzled. Participants also evaluate the accessibility of customer support for investment advice, reaching out for guidance on portfolio management and strategies. The ability to understand and execute trades seamlessly is vital, as users must feel confident navigating the investment landscape.

When the session wraps up, the young adult compiles the feedback, creating a detailed overview of each app's strengths and weaknesses. The room buzzes with discussion as friends share their experiences and insights, each contributing to a deeper understanding of the digital tools available to them. A sense of accomplishment arises from conducting a thorough evaluation that will inform their financial app choices.

Yet, as they reflect on the day's findings, a sense of unease emerges. Despite the wealth of information gathered, a lingering question remains: Are these digital tools truly secure? Recent headlines about data breaches and cyber threats come to mind, prompting them to consider whether the convenience of digital money management compromises privacy and security. The implications of trusting sensitive financial information to these apps are significant, as a single vulnerability could lead to serious consequences.

As the evening winds down, uncertainty lingers. The appeal of financial independence through digital tools is strong, yet the potential risks are considerable. The young adult resolves to further investigate the security measures of each app, determined to uncover the realities behind the polished interfaces and user-friendly designs. The pursuit of financial growth is filled with challenges, and they are ready to tackle the complexities ahead. What they discover next could have significant implications, leaving them to ponder: Is the digital age of money management a valuable opportunity or a risky endeavor?

Chapter 6: Saving Strategies for Small Budgets

In the organized space of a home office, a young adult is dedicated to mastering the principles of saving while working with a limited budget. This room serves as a hub for financial activities, featuring a collection of books neatly arranged on a shelf, a laptop running financial planning software, and a whiteboard clearly outlining specific saving goals in **bold** lettering, showcasing a commitment to achieving financial growth and independence.

The journey begins with establishing an **emergency fund**, a crucial financial safety net that provides security during unexpected expenses. Research indicates that a practical initial goal is to save an amount equivalent to three months' worth of living expenses. This requires a careful breakdown of monthly costs, including:

- rent
- utilities
- groceries
- other essentials

By multiplying total monthly expenses by three, a concrete target for the emergency fund is set. To maximize growth, the young adult explores online savings accounts that offer competitive interest rates and no maintenance fees, comparing various options to find the best fit. The **future value formula** helps project potential growth:

$$\text{Future Value} = \text{Principal} \times (1 + \text{Interest Rate})^{\text{Number of Years}}$$

This calculation allows for a clear visualization of how savings can grow over time, highlighting the importance of choosing the right account.

Next, **automated savings** are established, ensuring regular contributions to the savings account by setting up automatic transfers from the checking account to a designated savings account, committing to save a specific amount each week. This strategy leverages the power of consistency, as even small, regular contributions can add up significantly over time. A budgeting app aids in tracking progress, enabling adjustments to the savings rate as needed to stay on target.

While exploring **micro-investing platforms**, the young adult discovers opportunities to invest spare change from everyday purchases. These platforms round up transactions to the nearest dollar and invest the difference, making investing accessible even with limited funds. Potential returns and associated risks are carefully considered, opting for a diversified investment strategy to spread risk across various asset classes, aiming for a balance between potential returns and the inherent risks of investing.

The **cash envelope system** offers another effective saving technique. By allocating a specific amount of cash for different spending categories each month, greater control over finances is achieved. This method requires manual tracking of expenses, reinforcing financial discipline and revealing areas where savings can be made. The physical act of handling cash creates a tangible connection to spending habits, making it easier to identify and cut unnecessary expenses.

To enhance the saving strategy, **couponing** and **cashback apps** are utilized, providing discounts and cashback on everyday purchases, creating opportunities to save on routine expenses. Mastering the art of stacking discounts allows for maximizing savings by strategically planning purchases around sales and promotions. This proactive shopping approach not only reduces costs but also fosters a sense of accomplishment in securing the best deals.

Community resources play a vital role in financial development. Participating in local workshops focused on financial literacy and saving strategies offers valuable insights and networking opportunities. Engaging with peers encourages the exchange of tips and resources, creating a supportive environment for financial growth. Exploring community programs that provide discounts or financial assistance for essential services can further alleviate financial pressures.

A **vision board** in the office serves as a constant reminder of long-term financial goals, such as traveling or buying a home. Using visualization techniques helps maintain motivation, with regular updates to the board that reflect progress and new goals, reinforcing commitment to saving and outlining a clear path toward financial independence.

As these strategies are evaluated, it becomes evident that effective saving is not about the size of the budget but rather the consistency and creativity applied in its management. With a well- defined plan and the right tools, the young adult is on a promising path to establishing a secure financial future, steadily progressing toward their goals.

Chapter 7: Building Wealth with Micro-Investing

The young adult, driven by curiosity and determination, sits at their desk with a laptop open, ready to dive into the world of micro-investing. The room is quiet, with only the soft hum of the computer breaking the silence as they begin a thorough analysis of various platforms. This effort goes beyond casual exploration; it's about understanding how to build wealth from a modest capital base.

The analysis kicks off with a detailed spreadsheet comparing popular micro-investing options like **Acorns**, **Stash**, and **Robinhood**, each offering unique features assessed against several key metrics. **Fees** are a major consideration, as they can significantly impact returns, especially when starting with a limited investment. The young adult carefully documents:

- Monthly fees

- Transaction fees
- Any hidden charges that might not be immediately obvious

Investment options are another crucial factor. **Acorns**, for example, is known for its round-up feature, which automatically invests spare change from everyday purchases, making it especially appealing for those who want to start investing without a large initial deposit. In contrast, **Stash** offers a more personalized approach, allowing users to select investments that align with their interests and values, while **Robinhood** stands out with its commission-free trades, attracting those keen on directly trading stocks and ETFs.

The user interface of each platform is also critically evaluated, as a clean, intuitive design can simplify the investment process, making it more accessible and less intimidating for beginners. The young adult pays close attention to how easy it is to navigate the app, execute trades, and access account information, while also considering the availability of mobile applications since managing investments on the go is a priority for many young investors.

To gain a deeper understanding of each platform, the young adult consults user reviews and testimonial videos, which provide valuable insights into real experiences and highlight both the benefits and potential drawbacks. They focus on feedback regarding **customer service**, as responsive support is essential when addressing financial issues. Testimonials often reveal how platforms handle challenges like technical glitches or account discrepancies, which can be deciding factors in the selection process.

Educational resources offered by these platforms also receive attention. The young adult explores webinars, tutorials, and articles that cover investment fundamentals and strategies, as these resources are vital for establishing a solid foundation in investing, particularly for newcomers. Platforms that provide extensive educational content are more likely to empower users to make informed decisions.

Risk assessment plays a vital role in the research, as the young adult understands that investing inherently involves some level of risk, and aligning choices with their risk tolerance is crucial. Factors such as age, financial goals, and investment timeline significantly influence risk tolerance, so they utilize online assessment tools to gauge comfort levels with various types of investments, ranging from conservative bonds to more volatile stocks.

After thorough research and analysis, the young adult is ready to make an initial investment decision. They choose a platform that aligns with their financial goals and risk profile, feeling confident in their ability to start growing wealth, even with a small initial capital. This decision comes after careful consideration and a commitment to continuous learning and adaptation while navigating the landscape of micro-investing. With their chosen platform, they are prepared to take the first step in their investment journey, eager to see how their small investment can appreciate over time.

The young adult, now focused on building a diversified micro-investment portfolio, is surrounded by detailed notes and analytical graphs, each illustrating a specific aspect of the financial landscape they are eager to explore. **Asset allocation** is key to their strategy, as they learn to distribute investments among various asset classes, including stocks, bonds, and exchange-traded funds (ETFs), to effectively balance risk and return. This process involves understanding the **risk-return trade-off**, where higher potential returns typically come with increased risk. By strategically allocating assets across different investment types, they can reduce overall risk while optimizing potential gains.

The analytical tools offered by their chosen investment platform allow for customization of the portfolio based on a thorough risk assessment. This involves selecting a mix of aggressive and conservative investments tailored to their individual risk tolerance and financial goals.

- Aggressive investments, such as growth stocks, offer opportunities for higher returns but come with greater volatility.
- Conservative options, like government and corporate bonds, provide more stability and generally yield lower returns.

The young adult carefully evaluates their investment horizon and financial objectives, ensuring that the portfolio reflects a balance that aligns with their risk appetite and long-term aspirations.

Sector analysis is a vital part of the investment strategy, as various sectors, including technology, healthcare, and renewable energy, are examined for growth potential and relevance to personal interests. The technology sector, known for rapid innovation and significant global influence, presents substantial return opportunities, while healthcare is valued for its stability and resilience, especially during economic downturns. Renewable energy, driven by growing environmental awareness and supportive government policies, offers long-term growth prospects as the global economy shifts toward sustainable practices. Diversifying investments across these sectors allows them to capitalize on growth opportunities while minimizing exposure to sector-specific risks.

Establishing a systematic investment strategy for regular contributions is another important step. The young adult commits to recurring monthly investments through a method called *dollar-cost averaging*, which involves investing a fixed dollar amount at consistent intervals, regardless of market fluctuations. This approach helps mitigate the effects of market volatility by spreading the investment over time, potentially lowering the average cost per share. Committing to consistent contributions supports steady portfolio growth, harnessing the power of compounding to enhance returns over the long term.

Monitoring and rebalancing the portfolio is an ongoing process that requires regular evaluations to assess performance and make necessary adjustments. Scheduled reviews analyze how investments are performing in relation to financial goals and current market conditions. **Rebalancing** involves realigning the portfolio to its intended asset allocation, which may have shifted due to market movements. This process could include selling assets that have exceeded expectations and purchasing those that have underperformed to maintain the desired risk profile. Staying proactive and flexible allows for adaptation to market changes and shifts in personal financial circumstances, ensuring that the investment strategy consistently aligns with their objectives.

Engaging in the dynamic world of micro-investing, the young adult finds themselves immersed in lively discussions within online forums and social media groups, buzzing with activity and rich in knowledge and diverse perspectives. They actively participate in conversations, seeking advice from experienced investors while sharing their own insights. These forums are invaluable resources for learning about emerging market trends, innovative strategies, and the latest analytical tools that can enhance their investing practices.

Building a network with peers is crucial for their growth, as virtual meetups and webinars create opportunities to connect with other young investors who share similar financial aspirations. These interactions go beyond mere exchanges of tips; they focus on establishing a support network that encourages mutual growth and accountability. Through these connections, the young adult gains access to a wider array of ideas and methodologies, deepening their understanding of the micro-investing landscape.

Dedicated to continuous learning, they subscribe to various financial podcasts, newsletters, and online courses to stay updated on market trends and evolving strategies. Each podcast episode and newsletter article provides a new perspective, while online courses offer structured learning experiences that enhance their financial knowledge. This ongoing education is not just about collecting information; it aims to foster a mindset that embraces change and innovation.

A key part of their development involves creating a feedback loop, as they regularly assess their investment decisions and outcomes, analyzing which strategies were effective and which were not. This reflective practice allows them to refine their approach, making informed adjustments based on past experiences. By examining both successes and setbacks, they cultivate a more nuanced understanding of **risk management** and **strategic planning**.

Recognizing milestones serves as a powerful motivator, as each achievement, whether reaching a specific savings goal or seeing a positive return, reinforces their commitment to financial objectives. These celebrations not only acknowledge success but also highlight the progress made and the potential for future growth. Each milestone serves as a reminder of the opportunities that lie ahead, fueling their determination to keep pursuing their goals.

However, as they delve into the complexities of micro-investing, a sense of unease begins to emerge. Despite the wealth of knowledge and support available, a lingering question persists: Are they truly prepared for the complexities and uncertainties of the financial markets? Recent discussions in the forums about market volatility and economic downturns raise concerns about the stability of their portfolio, leading the young adult to question whether their strategies are robust enough to handle potential challenges.

Sitting at their desk, surrounded by notes and analytical graphs, a new realization dawns: the digital tools and strategies they've adopted are effective, but they do have limitations. The financial landscape is ever-changing, and the associated risks are very real. This awareness creates a sense of urgency, prompting them to consider whether any critical aspects of their strategy have been overlooked.

In this moment of reflection, the young adult faces an important decision: should they continue with their current strategies, or is it time to explore new options and seek additional guidance? The uncertainty feels significant, casting doubt over their achievements. As they contemplate their next steps, the stakes have never been higher, with the path ahead filled with potential challenges and an uncertain outcome. The future could greatly impact their financial well-being, leaving them to ponder: Are they truly ready for the challenges that lie ahead?

Key Takeaway

Starting your investment journey with micro-investing platforms is about more than just picking an app—it's about understanding fees, risk, and your own goals. Consistent learning, regular reviews, and a supportive network are essential for long-term financial growth.

Investing Scenarios with 10€, 100€, and 1000€

Seated at their desk, the young adult finds themselves surrounded by a collection of financial books and digital tools, each offering specific strategies for achieving financial growth. The task involves analyzing practical investment scenarios with minimal capital, starting with an initial amount of **10€**. This exploration of micro-investing begins with savings round-up apps, which automatically round up daily purchases to the nearest euro, directing the spare change into diversified investment funds. This method, while modest, serves as an effective introduction to investing and emphasizes the importance of habit formation along with the educational benefits of consistent, albeit small, contributions. With an initial investment of **10€**, growth will be incremental; however, the focus remains on cultivating a disciplined approach, which is essential for achieving long-term financial success.

Next, they investigate **fractional shares**, an innovative strategy that allows individuals to buy small portions of high-value stocks, enabling participation in the market without requiring substantial capital. Researching platforms that facilitate these purchases reveals the opportunity to own a stake in companies that were previously financially inaccessible. This democratization of stock ownership fosters a sense of inclusion in the financial markets and provides a practical learning experience. The realistic outcome of investing **10€** in fractional shares centers on gaining market exposure and understanding its underlying dynamics rather than expecting immediate financial returns.

With **100€**, the young adult explores more significant investment opportunities, one viable option being low-cost **exchange-traded funds (ETFs)**, which provide broad market exposure and diverse sector representation. ETFs attract attention due to their capacity for instant diversification, helping to mitigate the risks associated with investing in individual stocks. They meticulously evaluate various ETFs, considering factors such as:

- Expense ratios
- Historical performance
- Sector allocation

This thorough research proves critical in selecting an option that aligns with their financial objectives and risk tolerance.

Another compelling choice with **100€** involves **peer-to-peer (P2P) lending**, allowing them to lend to individuals or small businesses through P2P platforms, potentially achieving higher returns compared to traditional savings accounts. They remain aware of the associated risks, including borrower default, and manage these by diversifying lending across multiple borrowers while conducting careful assessments of each borrower's creditworthiness. The realistic outcome of investing **100€** in P2P lending presents the potential for moderate returns over a year, with the added advantage of reinvesting earnings to compound growth.

With **1000€**, the young adult can construct a more diversified portfolio, involving a strategic mix of stocks, bonds, and ETFs to achieve balanced risk management. They utilize investment calculators to model various scenarios, appreciating the increased flexibility and growth potential that accompany this level of capital. By strategically allocating investments, they aim to optimize returns while minimizing risk. They also consider investing in small businesses or startups through specialized platforms, which, while carrying higher risk, present the potential for substantial returns, particularly if the business thrives.

Throughout these scenarios, the young adult identifies user-friendly platforms with low fees and comprehensive educational support, which are crucial for novice investors as they equip them with the tools and resources necessary to make informed decisions. They stress the importance of establishing clear financial goals for each investment level, and planning regular reviews to monitor progress and adjust strategies as needed ensures that activities align with evolving financial objectives.

Reflecting on these scenarios, the young adult acknowledges that investing with small capital transcends mere financial gain; it involves building a solid foundation of knowledge, developing disciplined habits, and gaining confidence in their ability to navigate the financial markets. With each decision, they advance toward achieving financial independence and growth, equipped with practical strategies and digital tools essential for success.

Understanding Investment Risks and Rewards

Sitting at their desk, the young adult is ready to dive into the world of investment risks and rewards, armed with a notepad and pen. The goal is to break down these concepts into clear, relatable terms, making them easy to understand and practical for anyone starting their financial journey. Grasping **investment risk** is crucial, as it represents the chance of losing part or all of the initial investment, which can vary widely across different types. For instance, a 70% chance of rain suggests a strong likelihood of needing an umbrella, just as a higher investment risk means being prepared for possible financial losses.

Investment risks come in various forms, each with unique traits:

- **Market risk**: the potential for investments to lose value due to market fluctuations. Picture the stock market as a roller coaster, where rapid ups and downs can lead to unexpected changes in value.
- **Credit risk**: the chance that a borrower might not repay a loan, similar to lending money to a friend with the hope they'll pay you back, while also recognizing the risk they might not.
- **Liquidity risk**: the difficulty of selling an investment quickly without significantly lowering its price, much like owning a rare collectible that may take time to find a buyer willing to pay its full worth.

Understanding **rewards** is just as important, as they represent the potential returns or profits from an investment. Think of it like nurturing a young tree—small at first, but with proper care and time, it grows and provides shade and fruit. The key is to strike a balance between risks and rewards, which involves understanding the **risk-reward ratio** that assesses the relationship between potential risks and rewards, aiming for investments that align with individual risk tolerance. It's like choosing between a safe, well-paved path (low risk, low reward) and a steep mountain trail (high risk, high reward).

For beginners, practical strategies can greatly improve the investment experience. Consider the following approaches:

1. Start with a small amount: This allows for a better understanding of risk without facing significant financial repercussions.
2. Diversification: Spread investments across various asset classes to lower overall risk, much like maintaining a balanced diet by including different food groups for optimal health.
3. Regularly monitor investments: This enables timely adjustments to strategies as market conditions shift, while ongoing education about trends and options is also crucial for making informed decisions.

Reflecting on personal risk tolerance and financial goals is an important step in setting realistic expectations for growth. Regularly reviewing and adjusting strategies to align with evolving financial knowledge and life circumstances helps ensure that goals remain attainable. Understanding these fundamental concepts empowers the young adult and equips them to make informed decisions, confident in their ability to navigate the complexities of the financial landscape.

Chapter 8: Avoiding Common Money Mistakes

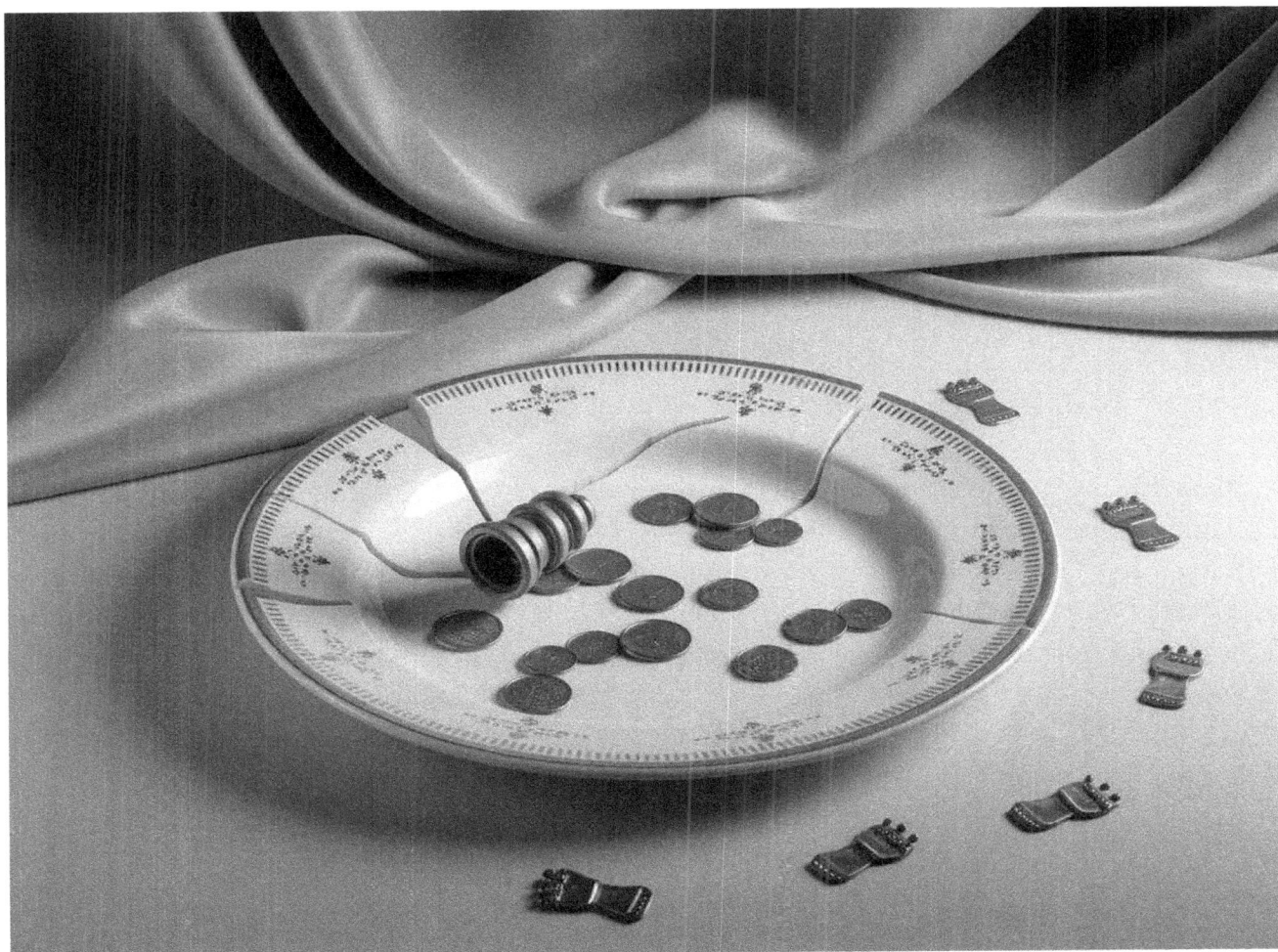

Sitting in a corner of their favorite café, the young adult, now equipped with foundational investment knowledge, is determined to build a solid financial foundation by learning from others' missteps. They sip their coffee while diving into research about common money mistakes that can hinder financial growth. The first pitfall they encounter is **impulse spending**, a habit that can quickly derail even the most carefully planned budget. This behavior involves making spontaneous purchases without prior planning, often driven by emotions rather than necessity. For example, buying a trendy gadget on a whim can lead to regret later when it disrupts their budget, and this tendency can accumulate over time, creating a significant dent in one's finances.

To combat impulse spending, the young adult learns the importance of practicing **mindful spending**, which means pausing for at least 24 hours before making a purchase to evaluate whether it fulfills a genuine need or is merely a fleeting desire. Distinguishing between needs and wants allows for more informed decisions, ensuring that spending aligns with financial goals.

Next, they explore the danger of **lifestyle inflation**, a common trap where increased income leads to higher spending on non-essential items. For instance, receiving a raise might tempt someone to upgrade to a luxury car instead of saving or investing the extra money. This pattern can prevent individuals from building wealth, as expenses rise in tandem with income, leaving little room for savings or investments. The young adult recognizes the importance of maintaining a modest lifestyle, even as income grows, to ensure that at least 20% of earnings can be allocated toward savings and investments.

Neglecting **emergency savings** is another critical mistake that leaves individuals vulnerable to unexpected expenses. Without an emergency fund, a sudden car repair or medical bill can lead to financial strain. Understanding that building such a fund is essential provides a safety net that can prevent setbacks. They aim to save at least three to six months' worth of living expenses, ensuring preparedness for unforeseen circumstances.

Misunderstanding **credit** and **debt** can be financially crippling. Mismanagement of credit cards and accumulating high-interest debt can lead to a cycle that's hard to escape. Treating a credit card like free money can result in overspending and mounting debt. The young adult learns the importance of using credit responsibly by paying off balances in full each month to avoid interest charges and understanding the terms and conditions of any credit agreements, including interest rates and fees.

Ignoring **budgeting** and tracking expenses is another common mistake. Without a budget, it's easy to lose track of where money is going, leading to overspending. Committing to creating a detailed budget, they categorize income and expenses to ensure they stay on course toward financial goals. Planning to review this budget monthly allows for adjustments based on changes in income or expenses.

Overlooking the importance of **financial education** can result in poor money management decisions. A lack of financial literacy can lead to confusion and mistakes in managing investments and savings. Recognizing the value of continuous education, the young adult regularly updates their financial knowledge through books, online courses, and credible financial news sources.

As they finish their coffee, the young adult feels more prepared to manage finances with awareness and caution. Implementing strategies to avoid common pitfalls ensures steady financial growth. They focus on the following key actions:

- Creating a budget
- Building an emergency fund

- Setting specific financial goals
- Continuously educating themselves
- Practicing mindful spending

These strategies equip them to make informed decisions and achieve financial confidence and growth.

Chapter 9: Building Credit and Trust with Banks

Understanding credit scores is a vital step in building a strong financial foundation. These scores act as numerical indicators of your **creditworthiness** and significantly influence your access to various financial products and services. Typically ranging from 300 to 850, higher scores indicate a lower risk to lenders and are based on several key factors that reflect your financial behavior.

Payment history is one of the most important components, making up about 35% of your overall score. It evaluates your reliability in making timely payments on all financial obligations, including credit cards, loans, and utility bills. Late payments can have a serious negative impact on your score, signaling a higher risk to potential lenders. To maintain a positive payment history, make sure to pay all your bills by their due dates. Consider the following strategies to help you avoid missing deadlines:

- Set up automatic payments
- Use calendar reminders
- Regularly check your payment schedules

Credit utilization is another essential factor, accounting for roughly 30% of your score. This ratio compares your current credit card balances to your total credit limits. Keeping your credit utilization ratio below 30% shows responsible management. For example, if you have a credit card with a $1,000 limit, aim to keep your balance at or below $300. High utilization can suggest an over-reliance on credit, which may raise concerns for lenders.

The length of your credit history contributes about 15% to your score. Generally, a longer history can enhance your score, as it provides lenders with more comprehensive data to assess your financial behavior. Therefore, it's often a good idea to keep older credit accounts active, even if you don't use them frequently. Closing these accounts can shorten your credit history and potentially lower your score.

Having a variety of credit accounts can also positively influence your score, accounting for about 10% of the total. A diverse mix of credit types, such as revolving credit cards, installment loans, and retail accounts, demonstrates your ability to manage different forms of credit responsibly. However, it's important to pursue only the credit that is necessary and manageable within your financial situation.

Recent credit inquiries can affect your score, making up the remaining 10%. When you apply for new credit, lenders perform a hard inquiry on your credit report, which can temporarily lower your score. Frequent inquiries may signal to lenders that you are seeking more credit than you can handle, raising red flags. It's wise to space out applications and apply for new credit only when absolutely necessary.

A good credit score is more than just a number; it opens the door to various financial benefits. With a high score, you're more likely to get approved for loans and credit cards, often with lower interest rates. This can lead to significant savings over time, especially on large loans like mortgages or auto loans. A strong score can also result in better insurance rates and increased negotiating power with lenders, allowing you to secure more favorable terms.

Consider two individuals applying for the same loan, one with a score of 750 and the other with a score of 650. The person with the higher score is likely to qualify for a lower interest rate, resulting in reduced monthly payments and less interest paid over the life of the loan. This difference can add up to thousands of dollars in savings, highlighting the financial importance of maintaining a good credit score.

Building and improving your score requires strategic actions. One effective method is to obtain a **secured credit card**, which requires a small deposit as collateral. This type of card is an excellent tool for establishing or rebuilding credit, functioning similarly to a traditional card but with less risk for the lender. Using it wisely and paying off the balance in full each month can gradually enhance your score.

Timely bill payments are another crucial aspect. Late payments can have a negative effect, so it's essential to set up reminders or automate payments to avoid missing due dates. Keeping credit card balances low is equally important, as high balances can increase your credit utilization ratio and negatively impact your score.

Regularly monitoring your credit reports is vital for ensuring accuracy. Errors can harm your score, so it's important to review your reports consistently and dispute any inaccuracies you find. You're entitled to a free report from each of the three major credit bureaus—*Equifax*, *Experian*, and *TransUnion*—once a year, which you can access through *AnnualCreditReport.com*.

Diversifying your credit types can also help build a strong history. Consider obtaining small installment loans or retail credit cards to enhance the variety in your profile. However, it's essential to manage these accounts responsibly and avoid taking on more credit than you can effectively handle.

Building a strong relationship with a bank is key to achieving financial growth. Start by opening both a **checking** and **savings** account, which shows your financial responsibility and sets the stage for a deeper connection with the institution. Regular account activity is important, as it demonstrates that you are actively managing your finances. This can include:

- Setting up direct deposits from your employer
- Consistently transferring funds to savings
- Using your debit card for everyday purchases

Each of these actions helps build a trustworthy financial profile in the eyes of the bank.

Effective communication with bank representatives is crucial. Developing a rapport with these professionals can lead to personalized financial advice tailored to your unique situation. Scheduling regular meetings with an advisor can provide valuable insights into the best products and services for your needs. These interactions may also open doors to exclusive offers or reduced fees, as banks often reward loyal customers with better terms.

A strong **credit profile** is a significant asset for financial advancement, as a solid credit history increases your borrowing capacity and enhances your ability to negotiate terms. One practical strategy is to request a credit limit increase; with a consistent payment history, asking for a higher limit can lower your credit utilization ratio, positively impacting your score and making you more attractive to lenders.

Exploring loan opportunities is another path to financial growth. Low-interest personal loans can be used for investments or educational purposes, boosting your earning potential. When evaluating options, comparing interest rates and terms is essential to secure the best deal. A strong credit score can also serve as a valuable negotiating tool when seeking lower rates on existing loans, potentially leading to significant savings over the life of the loan.

Understanding your needs and the available financial products is vital. Low-interest credit cards are particularly beneficial for balance transfers or large purchases, providing a way to manage debt more effectively. Rewards programs can offer *cashback* or *travel points* that help offset expenses. When deciding between personal loans and credit cards, consider the interest rates and repayment terms; personal loans typically have fixed rates and terms, making them suitable for larger, planned expenditures, while credit cards offer flexibility for smaller, ongoing purchases.

During a meeting with a bank advisor, the young adult protagonist shares their financial goals and explores suitable credit options. The advisor, impressed by their improved credit standing and proactive banking relationship, suggests a personal loan with favorable terms to support a side business venture, equipping the young adult with the resources needed to pursue their entrepreneurial aspirations.

Upon leaving the bank, they feel a sense of achievement. However, stepping onto the bustling street introduces a new challenge; their excitement for the business venture is tempered by the realization that the financial landscape is always changing, and with growth comes inherent risks. The young adult reflects on whether they are adequately prepared for the complexities ahead, considering what unforeseen challenges they might face and whether their newly adopted strategies will hold up over time. The quest for financial independence is filled with uncertainty, and as they ponder these questions, a sense of anticipation lingers, encouraging them—and the reader—to explore the complexities that lie ahead.

Building and Improving Your Credit Score

Common Mistake

A frequent mistake when building credit is applying for too many credit accounts in a short period. Each application triggers a hard inquiry, which can temporarily lower your score and signal risk to lenders. Instead, apply only when necessary and space out your applications. This careful approach helps protect your score and demonstrates responsible credit management—key for long-term financial growth and trust with financial institutions.

Establishing a strong financial foundation begins with creating your credit profile, and obtaining a **secured credit card** is an effective way to kick off this journey. Unlike traditional credit cards, a secured card requires a cash deposit that acts as collateral, typically matching your credit limit. This setup lowers the risk for the issuer, making it easier for those with no credit history or those rebuilding their credit to qualify. When looking for secured credit cards, focus on options with:

- Low annual fees
- A straightforward application process

This approach allows you to build credit without incurring unnecessary costs.

Once you have your secured card, use it for small, everyday purchases to help establish a reliable payment history, which is a key factor in determining your credit score. For example, consider using the card for monthly subscriptions or grocery shopping, ensuring you can pay off the balance in full each month. This habit showcases responsible credit management and helps you avoid interest charges, which can quickly add up.

Another effective way to build credit is by becoming an *authorized user* on a family member's credit card. This means adding your name to their account, allowing you to benefit from their established credit history. While the primary account holder is responsible for payments, the account's activity is reported to the credit bureaus and appears on your credit report. This can significantly boost your score, especially if the account has a long history of on-time payments and low credit utilization. Choose a family member who manages their credit responsibly to ensure their habits positively impact your score.

Applying for a **credit-builder loan** is another practical option for those looking to establish or improve their credit. These loans are often available through credit unions or community banks and are specifically designed to help individuals build credit. The process involves borrowing a small amount of money, which is deposited into a savings account while you make regular payments. At the end of the loan term, you receive the funds. The main advantage is that each payment is reported to the credit bureaus, helping to create a positive credit history. This type of loan is especially beneficial for those who may not qualify for traditional credit products.

Monitoring and managing your credit is essential for maintaining and improving your score. Credit monitoring services can offer valuable insights into your credit health. Many services provide free or low-cost options that allow you to track changes in your score and set up alerts for any new inquiries or account changes. This proactive approach keeps you informed and enables you to address any potential issues quickly.

Regularly reviewing your credit reports is another important aspect of effective credit management. You are entitled to receive a free annual report from each of the three major credit bureaus— Equifax, Experian, and TransUnion. Analyzing these reports helps you spot inaccuracies or unfamiliar accounts that could negatively affect your score. If you find any discrepancies, it's important to dispute them promptly to ensure your report accurately reflects your financial behavior.

Maintaining a budget is also crucial for effective credit management. Keeping a close eye on your spending ensures that all bills are paid on time, which is vital for maintaining a positive payment history. *Budgeting apps* can be particularly useful in managing your finances, providing a comprehensive overview of your income and expenses to help you avoid overspending and ensure you have enough funds to meet your obligations.

Avoiding common pitfalls is key to protecting your score. One major pitfall is applying for multiple credit accounts in a short period, as each application results in a hard inquiry on your report that can temporarily lower your score. To minimize this risk, apply for credit only when necessary and space out your applications to lessen the impact on your score.

Using financial apps is a smart and efficient way to keep an eye on your **credit score**. Apps like **Mint** and **Credit Karma** provide real-time updates and detailed insights into your credit health. These tools let you track your score over time, giving you a clear picture of how specific financial behaviors, such as *payment history* and *credit utilization*, impact it. By customizing notifications, you can receive alerts for upcoming due dates and spending limits, which helps you manage your financial responsibilities effectively. This proactive approach keeps you informed about your status and empowers you to make data-driven decisions to maintain or improve your score.

Setting credit goals is essential for boosting your score. Begin by defining both short-term and long-term targets. For example, you might aim to raise your score by 50 points in the next six months, while a long-term goal could be reaching a score of 800 within two years. Regularly assess your progress and adjust your strategies as needed. This might involve:

- Increasing credit limits
- Consolidating existing debt
- Automating payments to ensure bills are paid on time

Increasing credit limits can be a powerful way to improve your score by lowering your **credit utilization ratio**. Contact your card issuers to request higher limits, making sure there are no additional fees or unfavorable terms associated with the increase. A lower utilization ratio, ideally kept below 30%, indicates to lenders that you manage credit responsibly. For instance, if your current limit is $5,000 and your balance is $1,500, your utilization ratio is 30%. Raising your limit to $7,500 would reduce it to 20%, which can positively influence your score.

Consolidating debt is another practical step to enhance your score. Consider using balance transfer cards or personal loans to combine high-interest debt. This approach simplifies your payment process and can lower overall interest costs, making it easier to manage. When consolidating, compare interest rates and terms to find the best deal, as a lower rate allows more of your payment to go toward the principal balance, speeding up repayment and improving your score.

Automating payments is key to maintaining a positive payment history, which significantly impacts your score. Set up automatic payments for all your bills to avoid missed deadlines. This ensures that payments are consistently on time, preventing late fees and negative entries on your report. For bills that can't be automated, use calendar reminders to keep track of manual payment deadlines. This disciplined approach helps build a consistent history, which is crucial for achieving a strong score.

Avoiding common pitfalls is vital for protecting your score. Don't close old accounts, as keeping them open helps maintain the length of your credit history. Use these accounts occasionally to keep them active, which positively contributes to your score. Be mindful of making only minimum payments on credit cards; while it may seem manageable, paying just the minimum can lead to higher interest costs over time. Aim to pay more than the minimum to reduce debt more quickly and enhance your score.

Staying informed about changes in credit policies and scoring models is essential for effective management. Boost your knowledge by attending financial literacy workshops or webinars, which offer valuable insights into the latest trends and best practices. This ongoing learning process equips you with the tools you need to make informed decisions regarding your credit and financial health.

Diversifying credit types is a smart strategy that can greatly improve your credit profile over time. Keeping a mix of at least three different credit types—such as two credit cards, one installment loan (like a car loan), and a retail account—shows lenders that you can handle various forms of credit responsibly. This variety can boost your credit score by 10-30 points with a balanced mix and offers a safety net against potential financial challenges. For example, managing a credit card with a $5,000 limit, a $15,000 car loan, and a retail account with a $1,000 limit, all with on-time payments and low balances, indicates a strong credit history. However, it's essential to manage these accounts wisely, ensuring timely payments and keeping credit utilization below 30% of your total available credit.

Regular financial check-ups are key to maintaining a good credit score. Just like you would schedule routine health check-ups, it's important to review your financial status and credit health every six months. This review should include:

- Checking credit reports for errors, such as incorrect account balances or late payment marks
- Assessing your credit utilization ratio
- Ensuring your financial plans align with your current life situation

Changes in your life, such as marriage, a new job, or major purchases like a home, can affect your finances. Adjusting your plans, like recalibrating your budget or increasing savings, helps you stay on track to achieve your credit and financial goals.

Long-term improvement strategies can further enhance your credit standing, and **negotiating better terms** with creditors is one effective approach. If you have a history of timely payments, consider reaching out to negotiate lower interest rates, which can lower monthly payments by 1- 3% and reduce the total interest paid over the life of the loan. Looking into refinancing options for existing loans can also lead to better terms, potentially saving you thousands of dollars and improving your credit score by lowering your debt-to-income ratio.

Investing in credit education is another important aspect of long-term management. Taking courses on credit management and personal finance, such as those offered by accredited institutions or online platforms, equips you with the knowledge to make informed decisions. Staying updated with financial news and trends through reputable sources helps you remain aware of any changes in credit policies or economic conditions that could impact your financial health.

Avoiding common pitfalls in long-term credit management is crucial, as neglecting changes in your score can be harmful. Being proactive in addressing any drops is important; investigate and resolve issues promptly, such as disputing inaccuracies with credit bureaus. It's also wise to avoid over-reliance on credit; while it can be a helpful tool, it shouldn't be your main financial resource. Maintaining a healthy savings buffer of at least three to six months' worth of living expenses is essential to prevent falling into a cycle of debt.

Life events can have a significant impact on credit, and underestimating their effects can lead to financial strain. Planning for major life events, such as buying a home or starting a family, is vital. Preparing for unexpected expenses, like medical emergencies or job loss, by setting aside an emergency fund can help you avoid relying on credit and safeguard your financial stability.

Navigating the complexities of long-term credit management requires an understanding that the financial landscape is always changing. Just when you think you've mastered credit management, a new challenge may arise. An unexpected economic downturn, a sudden change in interest rates, or a personal financial crisis can test your resilience and the strategies you've put in place.

Chapter 10: Side Hustles and Digital Income Streams

Tip

Start small and focus on one digital side hustle at a time. Master the basics, build your reputation, and gradually expand your offerings. Consistency and quality matter more than trying to do everything at once. Use digital tools to track progress and stay organized.

In today's digital world, the opportunity to earn extra income through side hustles is greater than ever. By using strategic methods, you can tap into various platforms to create a steady income stream, even with a small initial investment. This discussion will explore the landscape of digital side hustles and offer practical tips on how to find and make the most of these opportunities.

Freelancing platforms are a fantastic starting point for anyone looking to turn their skills into cash. Websites like **Upwork**, **Fiverr**, and **Freelancer** have become popular marketplaces for a wide range of services, including:

- writing
- graphic design
- programming
- digital marketing

Begin by evaluating your marketable skills and identifying which ones are in demand. Reflect on your strengths and how they can be transformed into a service. For instance, if you have a knack for writing, consider offering content creation or copywriting services. If graphic design is your specialty, you might focus on crafting logos or marketing materials for businesses.

Once you've identified your skills, the next step is to create an engaging profile on these platforms. Think of your profile as your digital storefront; it's crucial to showcase your expertise and past work effectively. Include a professional headshot, a detailed description of your services, and examples of previous projects, highlighting any relevant experience and unique skills that set you apart from others. Remember, potential clients will judge your abilities based on your profile, so make sure it's polished and professional.

Online tutoring and teaching are also great ways to earn money. Platforms like **VIPKid**, **Teachable**, and **Skillshare** allow you to offer courses or tutoring sessions in your areas of expertise. Whether you're proficient in a foreign language, music, or programming, there's likely a demand for your knowledge. To succeed in this field, set competitive pricing that reflects your expertise and the value you provide. Use social media and professional networks to promote your services and broaden your reach. Building a reputation as a knowledgeable and reliable tutor can lead to repeat clients and referrals.

E-commerce is another exciting avenue for generating digital income. Platforms like **Etsy**, **Amazon**, and **eBay** provide the infrastructure needed to sell products without a physical storefront. You can explore various business models, such as:

- dropshipping
- print-on-demand
- selling handmade items

Dropshipping allows you to sell products without holding inventory, while print-on-demand lets you create custom designs on items like t-shirts and mugs. If you enjoy crafting, selling handmade products on Etsy can be a rewarding venture. No matter which model you choose, establishing a strong brand presence and marketing strategy is essential. This includes creating a memorable brand name, designing an appealing logo, and crafting a compelling story that resonates with your target audience.

Building an online presence is vital for the success of any digital side hustle. **Social media marketing** is a powerful tool for reaching potential customers and clients. Platforms like Instagram, Facebook, and LinkedIn enable you to promote your services and engage with your audience through regular posts and interactions. Keeping a consistent posting schedule is important; frequent updates help keep your audience engaged and informed about your offerings. Collaborating with influencers can also expand your reach and introduce your services to new audiences.

Blogging and content creation are effective ways to boost your online presence. Starting a blog or YouTube channel focused on your expertise allows you to share your knowledge and passion with a wider audience. Monetization opportunities in this space include:

- ads
- sponsorships
- affiliate marketing

The key to success is consistently producing high-quality content and engaging with your audience. Regularly sharing valuable content builds trust and authority, attracting more followers and potential customers.

Maximizing your earnings through digital tools is crucial for managing a successful side hustle. Financial management apps like **QuickBooks** or **FreshBooks** can help you track income and expenses, giving you a clear picture of your financial situation. Setting specific financial goals and monitoring your progress keeps you focused and motivated. Investing in skill development is also important for staying competitive. Online courses, webinars, and workshops provide opportunities to enhance skills relevant to your side hustle. Keeping up with industry trends and adjusting your strategies accordingly will help you remain competitive in your field.

Exploring these digital side hustle opportunities requires dedication, persistence, and a commitment to continuous learning. The digital landscape is always changing, and being adaptable is key to thriving in this dynamic environment.

Effective scheduling is key to successfully managing a side hustle alongside a full-time job. Digital calendars and task management tools like **Trello** or **Asana** are invaluable for organizing your time. Begin by creating a detailed list of all tasks related to your side hustle, categorizing them by urgency and importance. Utilize the **Eisenhower Box** method to prioritize these tasks, which helps you differentiate between what's urgent and important, while also identifying tasks that can be delegated or postponed. This structured approach enables you to concentrate on high-impact activities, reducing distractions from less critical tasks.

Set realistic deadlines for each task, taking into account your available time and energy levels. Block out specific time slots in your calendar dedicated solely to side hustle activities. This might involve waking up an hour earlier or reserving several evenings each week for focused work on your project. Consistency is crucial; establishing a routine helps develop a habit that becomes easier to maintain over time.

Balancing a full-time job with a side hustle requires clear communication and boundary-setting. If your side hustle starts to interfere with your primary job responsibilities, have an open conversation with your employer. Clearly express your commitments and reassure them that your main job remains your top priority. This transparency can help prevent misunderstandings and create a supportive work environment.

To minimize the risk of burnout, make sure to incorporate regular breaks into your schedule. The **Pomodoro Technique**, which involves working in focused intervals of 25 minutes followed by a 5-minute break, can significantly boost productivity and maintain your energy levels. Prioritizing your well-being is essential for long-term success, so pay attention to your physical and mental state, and take time to recharge as needed.

Networking and community building are vital for growing your side hustle. Engaging with online communities relevant to your field, such as *Reddit* or *Facebook Groups*, allows you to share experiences and gain insights from others. These platforms are rich in knowledge and can provide valuable feedback on your services or products. Participate in virtual networking events to connect with potential clients and collaborators, as these interactions can lead to partnerships that enhance your offerings and broaden your market reach.

Collaborating with other entrepreneurs can open up new growth opportunities. Look for partnerships for joint ventures or projects that complement your skill set. Such collaborations can lead to innovative solutions and shared resources, resulting in cost savings and increased operational efficiency. Consider exchanging services with fellow entrepreneurs to expand your skill set and service offerings. Co-hosting webinars or workshops is another effective way to reach wider audiences and establish your authority in your field.

Scaling and diversifying income streams are crucial for long-term sustainability. Start by expanding your service offerings in response to market demand. Conduct thorough market research to identify gaps or emerging trends that align with your expertise. Implement cross-selling strategies to existing clients by introducing complementary services or products, thereby increasing revenue without needing to acquire new customers.

Automation and delegation are powerful strategies for scaling your side hustle. Use automation tools to handle repetitive tasks like email marketing or invoicing, freeing up time for more strategic initiatives. Consider hiring virtual assistants or subcontractors to support operations, allowing you to focus on growth and innovation.

Reinvesting profits is essential for business expansion. Set aside a portion of your earnings for marketing, equipment upgrades, or skill development. Explore passive income opportunities, such as digital products or licensing, which can create a steady revenue stream with minimal ongoing effort. Continuously assess and adapt your business strategies to ensure sustainable growth in an ever-evolving market.

As you navigate the complexities of managing a side hustle, remember that the digital landscape is always changing. Just when you think you've found a balance between work and entrepreneurship, new challenges may arise. A sudden shift in market trends or an unexpected technological advancement could disrupt your carefully laid plans. Are you ready to pivot and adapt, or will these changes catch you off guard? The journey toward financial independence is filled with uncertainties, and reflecting on these questions can spark anticipation about the developments that lie ahead in your digital entrepreneurship efforts.

Chapter 11: Protecting Your Money in the Digital Age

Tip

Protecting your digital finances starts with small, consistent actions. Use a password manager to create unique, strong passwords for every account, and enable two-factor authentication wherever possible. Always verify emails and links before clicking, especially those related to your finances. Regularly update your devices and software to patch vulnerabilities, and avoid public Wi-Fi for financial transactions unless you use a VPN. These habits build a strong foundation for your financial security.

In the digital age, safeguarding your finances means understanding the specific threats that exist online, with **cybersecurity risks** being among the most significant dangers. **Phishing attacks** are a common tactic used by cybercriminals to obtain sensitive financial information. These often appear as deceptive emails or messages that mimic legitimate sources, such as banks or financial institutions, urging you to click on a link or provide personal details. To protect yourself, always verify the sender's email address for authenticity and steer clear of suspicious links. If you have any doubts, reach out to the institution directly using a verified phone number or their official website.

Malware and **ransomware** present additional critical threats to your digital financial data. Malware can sneak onto your devices through seemingly harmless downloads or attachments, putting your information at risk. Ransomware, on the other hand, locks you out of your data until a ransom is paid. To minimize these risks, ensure your devices have up-to-date antivirus and anti-malware software, perform regular system scans for potential threats, and avoid downloading files from untrusted sources, which can serve as gateways for malware.

Public Wi-Fi and unsecured networks create further vulnerabilities for your financial security. Connecting to these networks can allow cybercriminals to intercept your data, leading to unauthorized access to sensitive information. To safeguard your data, use a **Virtual Private Network (VPN)** to encrypt your internet connection, especially when accessing financial accounts or conducting transactions online. A VPN creates a secure tunnel for your data, making it much harder for hackers to intercept your information.

Fraudulent schemes and scams are prevalent in digital environments, with *Ponzi schemes* and *pyramid scams* being particularly notorious for promising high returns with minimal risk, luring unsuspecting individuals to invest their money. To avoid falling victim, maintain a skeptical attitude toward any investment opportunity that seems too good to be true, and conduct thorough due diligence while consulting with trusted financial advisors before committing your funds.

Fake investment opportunities are another common scam, often promoted through social media platforms or unsolicited emails. These schemes typically promise quick profits but are designed to defraud investors. Always verify the legitimacy of an investment by checking with regulatory bodies such as the **Securities and Exchange Commission (SEC)** or the **Financial Industry Regulatory Authority (FINRA)** to ensure compliance.

Identity theft and unauthorized transactions remain significant concerns in the digital landscape. Cybercriminals can steal your personal information to make unauthorized purchases or open accounts in your name. To protect yourself, regularly monitor your financial accounts for any suspicious activity and report unauthorized transactions immediately. Consider placing a fraud alert or credit freeze on your credit reports to prevent identity thieves from opening new accounts under your name.

Building a secure financial foundation starts with effective password management practices. Use password managers to create and securely store complex passwords, ensuring that each account is protected by a unique password. Implement **two-factor authentication (2FA)** for all financial accounts, which adds an extra layer of security by requiring a second form of verification, such as a text message or authentication app, in addition to your password. Regularly update your passwords and monitor account activity for any signs of unauthorized access.

Securing your devices and networks is equally important. Keeping software and security patches current on all devices protects against vulnerabilities that cybercriminals may exploit. Install reputable antivirus and anti-malware software to detect and eliminate threats. When using public networks, always connect through a VPN to safeguard your data from potential interception.

Staying informed about digital financial security is essential. Subscribe to cybersecurity blogs and newsletters for timely updates on the latest threats and protective measures. Attend webinars and workshops focused on digital financial security to enhance your knowledge and skills. Follow reputable financial advisors and cybersecurity experts on social media to keep up with best practices and emerging trends.

Encryption and data protection are crucial for keeping your financial information safe in today's digital world. Consider using **encrypted email services** for sensitive communications; they use advanced algorithms to convert messages into unreadable formats that only the intended recipient can decode with a secure key. This method effectively blocks unauthorized access and maintains confidentiality. Additionally, storing sensitive documents in **encrypted cloud solutions** with end-to-end encryption provides extra security by protecting files during transmission and while stored. This way, even if a data breach occurs, your information stays secure.

Regularly backing up your data to secure locations is another important practice. Use external hard drives with **hardware encryption** or trusted cloud services that have strong security protocols to create copies of essential files. This approach protects against data loss from hardware failures or cyberattacks and allows for quick recovery in emergencies.

When it comes to secure financial transactions, opt for payment methods that offer robust fraud protection, like PayPal or credit cards with advanced security features such as **two-factor authentication**. These options often include buyer protection programs that help recover funds from unauthorized transactions. Before making online purchases, verify the legitimacy of vendors and platforms by checking for secure website indicators, such as:

- HTTPS in the URL
- Trust seals from recognized security organizations

Regularly monitor your bank and credit card statements for any unauthorized activities, and report any suspicious transactions to your financial institution promptly to minimize potential losses.

Establishing financial safety nets is equally important. Start by creating a digital emergency fund that you can access easily through secure channels. Calculate a realistic amount to cover unexpected expenses, such as medical emergencies or sudden job loss, and maintain this fund consistently while regularly contributing to and reviewing it to ensure it meets your needs.

Think about investing in **identity theft protection services** and insurance to shield against potential threats. These services monitor your personal information continuously and alert you to any suspicious activities, allowing for immediate action. If you run a digital business, evaluate **cyber insurance** options that cover losses from data breaches or cyberattacks, ensuring that your financial assets are protected by comprehensive policies that provide a safety net in unforeseen circumstances.

Developing a risk management strategy is essential for navigating the complexities of digital finance. Start by assessing your personal risk tolerance to understand your comfort levels with digital financial tools and their associated risks. Create a diversified investment portfolio to spread and mitigate risks, ensuring that your investments are not overly concentrated in a single asset or market. Regularly review and adjust your financial strategies based on ongoing risk assessments to adapt to changes in the market or your personal circumstances.

Having response plans for financial security breaches is crucial. Develop a detailed plan that outlines the steps to take in the event of identity theft or fraud, including keeping contact information for financial institutions and cybersecurity support readily accessible. Knowing how to respond quickly and effectively can minimize the impact of a breach and protect your assets.

While implementing these advanced security measures and financial safety nets, stay alert to the ever-evolving nature of digital threats. Just when you think you've strengthened your defenses, a new vulnerability may emerge, testing your preparedness. Are you truly ready to tackle emerging challenges, or will the next wave of cyber threats catch you off guard? The landscape of digital security is uncertain, and the stakes have never been higher. The future of financial security is dynamic and requires ongoing attention and adaptation.

Protecting Yourself from Digital Scams and Fraud

In today's digital world, where communication happens instantly across the globe, recognizing warning signs in digital messages is crucial for safeguarding your financial assets. Scammers often send phishing emails that begin with generic greetings like **"Dear Customer"** or **"Dear User,"** which should raise a red flag. Legitimate companies usually personalize their communications by using your full name. These emails often contain urgent requests, such as **"Your account will be suspended unless you verify your information immediately,"** designed to bypass your logical thinking and push you to act quickly without considering the potential risks.

Another important warning sign is inconsistencies in sender email addresses and domain names. Scammers frequently create addresses that closely mimic those of real organizations, making small alterations like replacing letters with numbers or adding extra characters. Always verify the sender's email address and domain name for authenticity; if anything seems off, it's best to proceed with caution.

Refrain from clicking on unfamiliar links or downloading unexpected attachments, as these actions can lead to malware infections or direct you to phishing sites aimed at stealing your personal information. If you receive an email with a link or attachment that you weren't expecting, reach out to the sender through a verified communication method to confirm its legitimacy.

Social media platforms can also be a breeding ground for scams, so be cautious with friend requests from unknown profiles, especially those promoting investment opportunities. Scammers often set up fake accounts that imitate legitimate businesses or financial advisors to gain your trust. Before engaging with any offers, consider the following:

- Look for official badges on profiles, which indicate that the platform has verified the account.
- Check reviews and testimonials from reputable sources to assess the legitimacy of the business or individual.

Unsolicited phone calls and text messages are common tactics used by scammers to extract personal information. If you receive a call from someone claiming to represent a financial institution, do not share any personal details. Instead, verify the caller's identity through official channels, such as contacting the institution's customer service number listed on their official website. If the call or text seems suspicious, report the number to your service provider and relevant authorities to help protect others from falling victim to the same scam.

When assessing the legitimacy of online financial offers, thorough research is essential. Start by checking the background of companies offering financial services and confirm their registration with official financial regulatory bodies, such as the *Securities and Exchange Commission (SEC)* or the *Financial Industry Regulatory Authority (FINRA)*. These registrations indicate that the company is subject to regulatory oversight and must adhere to specific standards.

Reading reviews and testimonials from credible sources can provide valuable insights into a company's reputation and reliability. Be wary of offers that promise high returns with minimal risk, as these are often unrealistic. Understanding the investment mechanism is vital; request detailed documentation and take the time to read and comprehend it thoroughly. If you have any doubts, consult with a trusted financial advisor before making any significant commitments.

Verifying payment methods and security is another crucial step in protecting yourself from scams. Use secure payment gateways, such as **PayPal** or credit cards that offer fraud protection, and avoid direct bank transfers to unfamiliar entities. Ensure that websites are secured with **HTTPS** and have valid security certificates, which indicate that the site encrypts your data to protect it from unauthorized access. Be cautious of requests for payment in cryptocurrencies or gift cards, as these are often exploited by scammers due to their untraceable nature.

Stay vigilant and skeptical as your primary defenses against scams and fraud. Recognizing warning signs and taking proactive steps to verify the legitimacy of communications and offers will help protect your financial well-being and lay a secure foundation for your future.

Setting up **alerts** and **notifications** is a crucial step in actively reducing the risk of digital scams. By enabling real-time alerts for transactions and account activities, you can receive immediate notifications whenever there's activity in your accounts, such as deposits, withdrawals, or transfers. This feature allows you to respond quickly if any transactions seem suspicious. Customize your notification settings to highlight unusual spending patterns, such as transactions that exceed a certain amount—*e.g.*, $100—or occur in unfamiliar locations. Regularly reviewing these alerts is important; it helps you catch unauthorized activities early, minimizing potential financial losses.

Establishing trusted contacts is another key strategy. Designating specific individuals for financial advice and second opinions can provide valuable guidance. Consider including:

- Family members
- Close friends
- Certified financial advisors who understand your goals

Sharing scam alerts and prevention tips within your network builds a collective defense against fraud. Creating a support system for exchanging experiences and resources enhances your protection and fosters a community that is more resilient against scams.

Continuous education is essential for staying ahead of scammers. Engaging in online courses focused on financial literacy and digital security deepens your understanding of these topics. Joining forums and communities dedicated to scam prevention allows you to learn from others' experiences and share your insights. Staying informed about emerging scam tactics and prevention strategies is vital, as scammers are always adapting their methods. Keeping yourself updated helps you better safeguard your financial assets.

If you fall victim to a scam, implementing effective response strategies is crucial. Immediate actions should include:

1. Reporting the incident to your financial institution and relevant authorities, which can aid in the potential recovery of lost funds and help prevent further fraudulent activities.
2. Changing all passwords and securing any compromised accounts.
3. Freezing your credit reports to prevent identity theft by blocking the opening of new accounts in your name.

Long-term recovery and prevention require ongoing vigilance. Regularly monitoring your credit scores and financial statements for any irregularities is essential. Implement additional security measures, such as **two-factor authentication (2FA)** and identity monitoring services, to create multiple layers of protection. Sharing your experience with others helps them recognize and avoid similar scams, turning your unfortunate experience into a valuable lesson for the community.

Seeking professional assistance can be beneficial in navigating the aftermath of a scam. Consulting with legal advisors can help you explore potential recovery of lost funds and understand your rights. Engaging with cybersecurity professionals for a comprehensive security review can identify vulnerabilities in your systems and strengthen defenses. If the emotional impact of the scam feels overwhelming, consider therapy or support groups to help process the experience and rebuild your confidence.

While navigating the complexities of digital finance, remember that the landscape is always changing. Just when you think you've fortified your defenses, a new threat may emerge, testing your preparedness. Are you truly equipped for the next wave of digital challenges, or will the evolving tactics of cybercriminals catch you off guard? The digital environment is filled with uncertainties, and the stakes are high. Reflecting on these considerations encourages a deeper exploration of financial security and a commitment to safeguarding your wealth. Enhancing your defenses is an ongoing process, and the next insight could significantly change your understanding of how to protect your financial future.

Chapter 12: Emergency Funds and Future Planning

Establishing an emergency fund is a vital step toward achieving financial stability and easing the stress that comes with unexpected expenses. This fund serves as a financial safety net, helping you manage unforeseen costs like **medical emergencies**, **job loss**, or **urgent home repairs**. Keeping this fund intact is important because it provides a cushion and reduces anxiety by ensuring you're prepared for the unexpected.

To figure out how much you need in your emergency fund, start by detailing your monthly expenses, including essential costs like:

- rent or mortgage
- utilities
- groceries
- transportation
- any other regular payments

Once you have a clear picture of your financial commitments, aim to save an amount that covers three to six months' worth of these living expenses. While this range is generally suggested, it's important to adjust your target based on your personal situation. For example, if you have a stable job with a steady income, three months' worth of expenses might be enough. However, if your job situation is less secure or if you have dependents, aiming for six months or more could be wiser.

Building an emergency fund takes discipline and a steady approach. Start by setting aside a fixed percentage of your income each month specifically for this purpose. Even if your initial contributions are small, making regular deposits is crucial. To make saving easier, consider setting up automatic transfers to a dedicated savings account just for emergencies. This strategy simplifies the saving process and reduces the chance of using the funds for non-emergency expenses. As your income grows or your expenses decrease, feel free to increase your contributions to help your fund grow faster.

Once your emergency fund is established, shift your attention to long-term financial planning. This involves setting clear goals, such as buying a home, traveling, or preparing for retirement. Break these goals into short-term, medium-term, and long-term targets, and regularly review and adjust your plan to reflect changes in your life and the economy.

Diversifying your savings and investment strategies is another key part of effective financial planning. Look into various options, such as **high-yield savings accounts**, **certificates of deposit (CDs)**, and **money market accounts**, to maximize your interest earnings. For potential growth, consider investing in **stocks**, **bonds**, and **mutual funds**. It's essential to balance your investment portfolio according to your risk tolerance and investment timeline to meet your financial goals while managing risk.

Preparing for major life events is also a crucial element of comprehensive financial planning. Anticipate and plan for milestones like:

- marriage
- childbirth
- educational expenses

Research insurance options that can protect you against unexpected life changes, and create a will along with an estate plan to ensure financial security for your beneficiaries.

Technology can greatly enhance your financial planning efforts. Use apps and tools to track your expenses and manage your cash flow effectively. Explore investment platforms that offer **robo-advisors** for personalized portfolio management, and utilize calculators for retirement planning and loan assessments. Staying informed and adaptable is key: subscribe to financial news sources to keep up with market trends, participate in webinars and workshops focused on financial planning and investment strategies, and engage with online communities to share insights and experiences.

Setting Up Your First Emergency Fund

Setting up your first **emergency fund** is a vital step in building a strong financial foundation. It acts as a safety net, providing peace of mind when unexpected expenses, like medical bills or car repairs, arise. The first step in this journey is to choose the right account for your emergency savings. A **high-yield savings account** is an excellent choice because it usually offers a much higher interest rate than traditional accounts, allowing your money to grow while still being easily accessible. This type of account keeps your funds safe and helps them increase over time.

When looking at high-yield savings accounts, it's important to ensure that the account is **FDIC insured**. This insurance protects your deposits up to $250,000, adding a crucial layer of security. In the unlikely event of a bank failure, your savings will be safe. Look for accounts with no or low fees, as even minor charges can eat away at your savings over time. Opting for an account that minimizes these costs is essential. Many online banks provide high-yield savings accounts with attractive interest rates and low fees, making them a smart option for your emergency fund.

Once you've chosen the right account, set your initial savings target. While experts often recommend saving three to six months' worth of essential expenses, starting from scratch can feel daunting. Instead, aim for a more achievable goal, like saving one month's worth of essential expenses. This makes the target feel more manageable. To figure out this amount, use a budgeting app to analyze your spending habits. These apps can help identify areas where you can cut back, allowing you to direct more money toward your emergency savings.

Creating a timeline for reaching your initial goal is also important. Break down the total amount into realistic monthly contributions. For example, if your goal is to save $3,000 in a year, plan to save $250 each month. This method simplifies the process and helps you stay focused.

Automating your savings is another effective strategy. Set up automatic transfers from your checking account to your emergency fund on payday to ensure regular contributions and reduce the chance of spending that money elsewhere.

As your financial situation changes, such as getting a raise or paying off debt, take the time to reassess and adjust your transfer amounts. Increasing your contributions as your income grows will help you reach your savings goal faster. Staying disciplined is key to successfully building an emergency fund. To avoid the temptation of dipping into the fund for non-emergencies, keep it in a separate bank from your main checking account. This creates a mental barrier that makes it less likely you'll use the funds for everyday expenses.

Making it a habit to review your emergency fund balance and progress each month keeps you motivated and allows you to track your journey toward your savings goal. Celebrate small milestones, like reaching 25% or 50% of your target. Recognizing these achievements reinforces positive financial habits and encourages you to keep saving.

Chapter 13: Measuring Progress and Adjusting Plans

Setting benchmarks for success is a vital step in managing your finances effectively. It involves defining specific milestones that align with both your short-term and long-term objectives. These benchmarks serve as reference points, guiding you through the complexities of achieving financial growth and stability. Begin by identifying immediate goals, such as:

- saving $2,000 for a vacation
- paying off a credit card debt of $1,500

Then, outline your long-term aspirations, like:

- accumulating a 20% down payment for a home purchase
- ensuring a retirement fund of $1 million

Establishing these targets creates a structured plan that keeps you focused and motivated.

Quantitative benchmarks are crucial for accurately measuring your progress. One effective method is to set percentage increases in savings or investment returns. For example, if your goal is to increase savings by **20%** over the next year, track your progress by calculating the monthly percentage increase needed to reach that target. This approach provides a clear numerical representation of your achievements, allowing you to assess how far you've come and what adjustments may be necessary. Monitoring the percentage growth of your investment portfolio, such as aiming for a **7%** annual return, can help you evaluate the effectiveness of your strategies.

Qualitative benchmarks capture broader aspects of success. Enhancing your financial literacy, for instance, is a significant milestone that can improve your ability to make informed decisions. Reducing financial stress serves as another qualitative benchmark that indicates a healthier relationship with money. These non-numerical indicators are just as important as financial figures, reflecting your overall improvement in well-being.

Regular financial check-ins are essential for maintaining your trajectory, so schedule monthly reviews of your financial statements, including:

- bank account balances
- investment performance
- monthly expenses

This practice enables you to monitor your progress and identify areas that need attention. Financial management apps or software can be particularly beneficial, as they generate detailed reports that highlight trends and potential issues. Conducting these reviews consistently allows you to make informed decisions and mitigate risks.

Quarterly assessments provide an opportunity to evaluate the effectiveness of your current strategies. During these evaluations, closely examine your goals and the specific actions taken to achieve them. Are your strategies yielding the expected results? Are there any changes in your situation, such as increased expenses or unexpected income, that necessitate adjustments? Addressing these questions ensures that your plan remains relevant and effective.

Adjusting your financial plan is a natural and necessary part of the process, so be ready to modify strategies based on fluctuations in income, expenses, or goals. For instance, if you receive a salary increase, consider allocating a portion to high-performing investments. If an investment is consistently underperforming, it may be wise to reallocate those funds to more promising opportunities. Updating your budget to reflect significant life changes, such as a new job, relocation, or changes in family size, is also crucial for maintaining stability.

Seeking feedback and advice can provide valuable insights into financial management. Consulting with a financial advisor can offer expert guidance tailored to your specific circumstances. Engaging with online communities allows you to share experiences and gain new perspectives on effective money management. Attending workshops or webinars keeps you informed about the latest tools and strategies, ensuring that you remain knowledgeable and proactive.

Recognizing progress and reassessing your goals are vital for sustaining motivation. Acknowledge and celebrate the achievement of key milestones, as this reinforces positive behaviors and encourages continued effort. Periodically reassess your financial goals to ensure they remain relevant and challenging as your situation evolves. Use your successes as a foundation to set more ambitious targets and gradually work towards greater independence.

Key Takeaway

Setting clear, measurable benchmarks—both quantitative and qualitative—is essential for tracking your financial progress. Regularly reviewing and adjusting your goals keeps you motivated and ensures your strategies stay effective as your life changes. Embrace digital tools for monitoring, seek feedback, and celebrate milestones to build lasting financial confidence. Remember, flexibility and consistent check-ins are key to long-term money management success.

Chapter 14: Beginner Success Stories and Lessons

Real-life experiences offer valuable lessons, especially in financial management. By examining the journeys of individuals who started with minimal capital, we uncover specific strategies and insights that are both practical and actionable. These stories reflect diverse backgrounds and motivations, providing unique perspectives on overcoming challenges and achieving success. They demonstrate that financial growth is within reach for anyone willing to learn and adapt.

Take, for example, a college student who began investing with just €50. Juggling a part-time job and academic responsibilities, this individual ventured into the investment world through micro-investing apps, allowing for the gradual creation of a diversified portfolio even with limited resources. Initial fears about market volatility were significant hurdles, but by using educational resources and sticking to a consistent investment strategy, the student achieved a **20% return** within a year. This success boosted confidence and inspired the student to share their knowledge with peers. The key takeaway here is the importance of starting small, staying consistent, and utilizing available educational tools to enhance financial literacy.

Next, we look at the financial management strategies of a freelance graphic designer facing unpredictable income. By using budgeting apps, this designer meticulously tracked expenses and prioritized savings, which was essential given the irregular income that required a disciplined approach to cash flow management, especially during lean times. Cutting unnecessary expenses and focusing on building an emergency fund allowed for the coverage of six months of living expenses, significantly reducing financial stress. This story highlights the importance of discipline, setting realistic financial goals, and the vital role that digital tools play in achieving stability.

Another compelling account is that of a young professional burdened with student loans and credit card debt. This individual adopted the **debt snowball method**, focusing on paying off the smallest debts first to build momentum. Staying motivated was challenging, particularly as income grew and the temptation of lifestyle inflation arose. However, celebrating small victories and concentrating on incremental progress enabled the young professional to eliminate all debt within three years and start investing €100 monthly. This transformation illustrates the psychological benefits of reducing debt and the effectiveness of recognizing small achievements to maintain motivation.

Finally, we explore the entrepreneurial journey of a high school student who started a small online business with an initial investment of just €10. By leveraging social media for marketing and reinvesting profits back into the business, the student achieved a **200% revenue increase** in the first year. Balancing academic responsibilities with business demands posed significant challenges, and initial setbacks were part of the learning curve. Nevertheless, persistence and the ability to learn from failures proved crucial. This story showcases the impact of digital platforms on business growth and the importance of resilience and adaptability in entrepreneurship.

These diverse narratives reinforce the idea that there are many pathways to financial growth. Each story emphasizes the importance of adaptability, continuous learning, and effectively using digital tools to navigate challenges and achieve success. By drawing practical insights from these experiences, readers can apply similar strategies in their own financial journeys, no matter where they start. The common thread in these stories is the belief that with the right mindset and resources, financial confidence and growth are attainable for everyone.

Chapter 15: Building a Confident Financial Future

Building financial confidence begins with adopting a proactive mindset. It's important to understand that growth is about more than just numbers; it involves actively managing your resources. By taking control of your situation, making informed decisions, and being willing to adjust your strategies based on new insights, you can navigate the financial landscape with confidence and resilience. A positive mindset can transform challenges into opportunities.

To lay a strong foundation for financial confidence, start by assessing your current situation. Create a personal financial statement that gives you a clear picture of your financial health. Begin by listing all sources of income, including your main salary, freelance work, and any passive income like dividends or rental income. Then, categorize your expenses into:

- Fixed expenses (like rent or mortgage payments)
- Variable expenses (such as groceries, dining out, and entertainment)

This detailed breakdown will help you see where your money goes and identify areas where you can save.

It's also essential to evaluate your assets and liabilities. **Assets** are anything of value you own, such as savings accounts, stocks, bonds, and real estate, while **liabilities** are your financial obligations, including credit card balances, student loans, and other debts. Calculating your **net worth**—by subtracting total liabilities from total assets—gives you a clear picture of your financial health, which is vital for making informed decisions.

Digital tools can greatly improve your ability to track and analyze your financial data. Apps like *Mint*, *YNAB* (You Need A Budget), and *Personal Capital* allow you to link your bank accounts, categorize transactions, and generate detailed reports. These tools provide a clear visualization of your financial status, making it easier to spot spending patterns and make informed choices.

Once you have a solid understanding of your financial situation, set specific goals categorized into:

1. Short-term goals (e.g., saving for a vacation or paying off a small debt)
2. Medium-term goals (e.g., buying a vehicle or building a solid emergency fund)
3. Long-term goals (e.g., purchasing a home or planning for retirement)

When setting these goals, use the **SMART** criteria: Specific, Measurable, Achievable, Relevant, and Time-bound. For example, instead of saying "save more money," a SMART goal would be "save $5,000 for a down payment on a car within the next 12 months." This structured approach provides clarity and direction, making it easier to track your progress and stay motivated.

Create a personalized financial plan to boost your confidence. Develop a realistic and flexible budget that aligns with your goals. This budget should include all income sources and prioritize essential expenses, such as housing, utilities, and groceries, while also setting aside a portion for savings and investments to ensure steady progress toward your objectives.

Digital budgeting apps can simplify this process by automating expense tracking and providing insights into your spending habits. These tools help you identify areas where you can cut costs and reallocate funds toward your goals. Features like bill reminders and goal tracking help you stay on top of your commitments.

Prioritizing expenses and savings is crucial for maintaining stability. Start by distinguishing between needs and wants to ensure that essential expenses are covered first. Once your basic needs are met, direct funds toward your goals, such as building an emergency fund or contributing to a retirement account. This approach ensures you are making progress toward your objectives while enjoying a balanced lifestyle.

Establishing an emergency fund is a key part of your financial planning. This fund acts as a safety net, providing stability and peace of mind in case of unexpected expenses, like medical emergencies or job loss. To start an emergency fund, decide on a target amount that covers three to six months of living expenses. Begin with small, consistent contributions, even if it's just $10 or $20 each week. Over time, these contributions will add up, creating a buffer that protects you from unforeseen setbacks.

The peace of mind that comes with having an emergency fund is invaluable. It empowers you to face life's uncertainties with confidence, knowing you're prepared for potential challenges. Keep building your financial foundation, remembering that achieving confidence takes ongoing effort and flexibility. Stay focused on your goals, remain adaptable in your approach, and consistently work toward a secure future.

Thinking beyond immediate financial needs is crucial for achieving long-term stability and growth. While managing daily expenses is important, focusing on **wealth-building strategies** can significantly enhance your financial outlook. It's essential to conduct a thorough analysis of investment options that align with your specific goals and **risk tolerance**.

Investment vehicles like stocks, bonds, mutual funds, and ETFs offer a variety of opportunities for capital appreciation. Stocks represent ownership in a company, providing the potential for substantial returns, though they also come with higher volatility and risk. On the other hand, bonds are debt instruments issued by corporations or governments, generally yielding lower returns but offering a more stable risk profile. Mutual funds pool capital from multiple investors to create a diversified portfolio of stocks and bonds, providing a balanced approach. ETFs, or *exchange-traded funds*, function similarly to mutual funds but are traded on stock exchanges, offering liquidity and often lower expense ratios.

Evaluating your **risk tolerance** is essential when choosing the right investments, so it's important to assess your comfort level with potential fluctuations in value. A higher risk tolerance might encourage you to allocate a larger portion of your portfolio to equities, while a lower risk tolerance could lead you toward fixed-income securities or balanced funds. Digital investment platforms like Robinhood, E*TRADE, and Betterment make it easier to enter the market, allowing you to start investing with minimal capital and gradually expand your portfolio.

Building a diversified portfolio is key to minimizing risk and optimizing returns. Diversification means spreading investments across various asset classes and sectors to reduce the impact of underperformance in any single investment. For instance, if technology stocks decline, gains in sectors like healthcare or consumer goods can help offset those losses. Aim to maintain a mix of:

- Equities
- Fixed-income securities
- Alternative assets

that align with your risk tolerance and financial goals.

The principle of **compounding interest** is a powerful driver of long-term wealth accumulation. Reinvesting earnings enables your investments to generate returns not just on the initial principal but also on the accumulated interest. This compounding effect can lead to significant growth over time. For example, an investment of $1,000 at an annual return of 7% can grow to about $1,967 over a decade, showcasing the power of compounding.

Continuous financial education is vital for making informed decisions and staying updated on market trends. The financial landscape is always evolving, and ongoing learning helps you adapt effectively. Resources like online courses, webinars, and financial blogs offer valuable insights and updates. Engaging with communities or forums fosters peer support and collaborative learning, boosting your financial literacy and confidence.

Flexibility in financial planning is essential for navigating life's changes, whether you're facing a career transition, family growth, or unexpected expenses. Your strategy should remain adaptable. Regular reviews and necessary adjustments ensure that your plans stay relevant and effective. For instance, a salary increase may allow for greater contributions to your investment accounts, while welcoming a new family member could necessitate increased savings for future obligations.

Taking charge of your financial future is vital for fostering growth. By implementing the strategies and tools you've learned, you can build confidence and independence. Approach your planning with a proactive mindset, understanding that each decision you make brings you closer to your goals.

As you prepare for potential challenges, consider whether you're ready to handle unforeseen circumstances. Just when you start to feel secure in your knowledge and strategies, unexpected events may arise, threatening to disrupt your plans. Market fluctuations, new investment opportunities, or personal crises may require immediate attention. How will you respond? Will you adapt and thrive, or will this moment test your resolve and determination? The pursuit of independence is inherently uncertain, and the next phase of your planning will reveal the true extent of your resilience and resourcefulness.

www.ingramcontent.com/pod-product-compliance
Lightning Source LLC
Chambersburg PA
CBHW081745200326
41597CB00024B/4399